LEADING HIGH-PERFORMANCE TEAM

Coaching in the Asian Culture

LAURENCE AND ENG NEO

BP Coach Training Pte Ltd

Published by BP Coach Training Pte Ltd.
3 Temasek Avenue, Centennial Tower Level 21, Singapore 039190
Email: info@bpcoachtrain.com
Website: www.bpcoachtrain.com

ISBN: 978-981-11-7929-7 (paperback)

Printed in the United States of America.

To both our parents.

Without the love and sacrifice that you made to put us through our education, we will never be where we are today.

CONTENTS

Praise & Foreword   vii

Introduction   xv

1. It's Time   1

2. Coffee Chat   5

3. The Taxi Ride   11

4. Intelligent Retail Solution   15

5. Tricia   23

6. Building Trust   27

7. Aligned Goals and Vision   33

8. Managing Millennials   39

9. Empowerment   45

10. Creating Awareness   49

11. Active Listening   55

12.	Ways of Listening	61
13.	No Time	65
14.	Coaching	69
15.	Asking the Right Question	73
16.	Intent of Question	77
17.	Breakfast with Gary	83
18.	Growth Mindset	87
19.	Cadence	93
20.	Defence	97
21.	Second Class Citizen	101
22.	The Coaching Conversation	105
23.	Building on Differences	111
24.	Quiet Time	117
25.	Lifelong Learning	121
26.	Systems and Processes	125
27.	Asian Management Style	129
28.	Who Bears Responsibility	135
29.	Decision	141
30.	Party Time	145
	About the Authors	149
	References	153

♥

Praise for the Book

"Succinctly narrative with gripping relevance. The story-telling style provides realistic in-situ workplace context that a reader can readily relate to – a clever and effective way of presenting ideas that may otherwise be esoteric to many. The book is a relatively quick read, but packs practical and timely insights for leaders to transform themselves towards adopting the coaching mindset that is necessary to build high performance teams. A worthwhile and essential book for leaders or aspiring leaders."
— *Lawrence Yong, CEO, MoolahSense Pte Ltd*

"The story-telling format of this book makes for easy reading. The key take-aways and learning points are relevant whether you are leading a small team, a department or an organisation. And the leadership skills and mindset highlighted are essential for every leader. Employees deliver their best in a climate that is constructive, positive and empowering. In today's digital economy, social media plays a big role in defining success and virtual interactions have overtaken face-to-face interactions by leaps and bounds. Every physical interaction, face-to-face or on the phone has become precious and such opportunities should be best leveraged using coaching techniques.
Clearly, Laurence and Eng Neo have written this book based on their vast experience as leaders in their own

organisations, against the backdrop of an Asian country. Cultural nuances played a big part of the coaching techniques through out the book. "

— *Chye N. Chong*, *Managing Director, IBM Malaysia*

"A book relevant for today's SME Leaders, distinguished by its deep insight on the coaching principles and skills. This book clearly explains the difference between Asian Teaching, Mentoring and Coaching and how we can effectively coach people to bring out the best in them.
I really enjoyed reading every chapter and have benefited from reading this book especially the listening and powerful questioning skill in my role as a manager.
Good book to share with all leaders who aspire to improve their team members' performance."

— *Cynthia Nah*, *Finance Manager*
Broadcast Professional Pte Ltd

"This book, through its many scenarios and anecdotes, has painstakingly laid out the emerging challenges often faced by management of SMEs. John, the coach character, takes on these challenges head-on and through the process, displays many of his sensitivities and acumen in the way he goes about coaching the management team of IRS Pte Ltd, a typical SME set-up in Singapore (often described as a melting pot of Asian cultures and diversities). The very best coaching, especially in the Asian culture context, often happens when the coachee does not realise he or she is being coached. These are just a few of the many "aha" moments in this book that should send the lightbulbs flashing in the minds of every supervisor, manager or director.
The authors labelled their work as a fable. I would rather call it a down-to-earth, honest and realistic portrayal of

the growing struggles many of our Asian SMEs face. The book suggests that SMEs may not necessarily be always struggling from the lack of skilled talents or technical know-hows. Rather, what is sorely lacking are the capabilities needed to lead a high-performance team. Coaching, as the authors Laurence and Eng Neo have demonstrated in the book, can address many of these capabilities, and when embraced by SMEs, can bring about the transformational changes needed to survive an increasingly VUCA world."

— *Winston Tan, Trainer & Learning Consultant, Wellern International, Associate Trainer with Civil Service College, Singapore. He trains and inspires thousands of public officers in many countries through his programme.*

"A captivating and well written book on leadership coaching that exemplifies how to conduct coaching more professionally with practical emphasis. The explanation and guidance in the book on the coaching process are crystal clear and can be easily understood through the case scenario. I highly recommend this book to all leaders who have keen interest in the developmental aspects for their staff. This is a must read book for all leaders who would like to apply the coaching approach towards their staff development. I am sure you will benefit greatly from reading it!"

— *Francis Seah, Regional HR Business Partner Idemitsu International (Asia) Pte Ltd*

♥

Foreword

Leadership skill is a crucial life skill that is required by everyone who wants to succeed in life even when we are not working in a corporate environment. When one is working alone, he/she would also need self-leadership to manage, motivate and inspire himself/herself to achieve the goals. We know that the key leadership domains include communicating effectively to motivate others to achieve results, inspiring them to walk uncharted paths and helping them to unleash their full potential. These concepts are easily understood but difficult to practise.

More often than not, many organizations do not see the corresponding increase in their leadership effectiveness after sending their key talents for leadership training. So where is the shortfall? Even highly motivated employees can find it difficult to elevate their leadership effectiveness after attending a leadership workshop. The reason? They are held back by ineffective habits, disempowering beliefs and their own perception of reality. They are sometimes stifled by fear of potential embarrassment and anxieties.

So, if leadership training is only half the equation, what is the missing half? The gap is in leadership coaching. What is the difference? Training imparts knowledge while coaching helps leaders to internalize these new skills and behaviors through self-reflection, awareness and developing customized solutions to implement the leadership concepts. The support and encouragement offered by the coach can help these leaders increase their courage and confidence to experiment with new behaviors.

Many leaders have cognitive knowledge of what effective leadership entails but find it a challenge to translate this knowledge into effective behaviors. They say one thing but act in another manner. This may not be intentional. They are simply not aware of the misalignment due to the lack of awareness. We call them blind spots. Coaches working with these leaders help them to discover their blind spots and support them to make the necessary shifts.

The advantage of leaders being trained as a coach is two-fold. One, they understand and learn the techniques of empowering and engaging others to realize their capabilities. In doing so, many of such leader-coaches also apply the same methodologies to help themselves in the process.

Coaching is a life skill. It helps us as practitioners to elevate our self-leadership. It can also be used in our roles as parents, friends and/or work colleagues.

Those who are not trained as coaches tend to associate coaching with training or mentoring. They equate that word with their experiences with a sports coach, who teaches the techniques and nuances of the game. This is not coaching and unfortunately, coaching is not easy to master. Giving advice and solutions are what we naturally do to help others. Coaching on the other hand, is a facilitation skill to help others find their unique path and solutions for their challenges.

You might be curious as to why coaches do not provide solutions. Especially when you, as a coach, feel that you have one at hand to help the person facing the problem. The answer lies in the neuro-science of change. Permanent change only happens in the "aha" moment through self-reflection. Coaching provides this platform for people to achieve those insights.

In this book, you will understand the concepts of leadership and discover how coaching is an important ingredient in helping leaders develop high-performance team. There are loads of useful and powerful tips that can help you become a better leader and coach. I know that you will find valuable insights here that will enhance your leadership journey.

Wai K Leong
ICF[1] Master Certified Coach
ICF Global, Vice President (2017)
ICF Global, Director (2014 – 2018)
Author of Empowering Asian Mindsets through Coaching *and* Powerful Performance Coaching Tips

---

1. *ICF - International Coach Federation is a global organization that supports and sets the standards for professional coaching.*

INTRODUCTION

Welcome to a fulfilling and rewarding world of leadership. By picking up this book, it is a testament of your courage and desire to make a difference in your leadership journey. Leadership is a skill that can be learned through training, mindset shifts, observation, practice and experience. In other words, leaders are made and not born.

Leadership entails more than just putting in place systems, processes and managing people by rules and policies. In the VUCA (Volatile, Uncertain, Complex and Ambiguous) world that we operate in, it is essential to have High-Performing Leaders—Leaders who have the right mindset and attitude to navigate challenges and capabilities to lead their teams to great heights.

Some of you were probably promoted to a manager because of your past commitment and performance as an individual contributor. As a manager, you may have the same level of expectation of your team. Lo and behold, you start to find that a certain team member, Peter, seems indifferent about missing deadlines, or Mary simply has no accountability when it comes to meeting client's expectation. Sounds familiar?

Perhaps, you may have been externally hired to manage a department within an organization. A client of ours who was headhunted for a senior position shared her challenges managing her team during a coaching conversation. She used buttons as a metaphor by depicting herself as an odd brown button among a mix of colorful ones—A feeling of being out of place with a culturally diversified team which she had inherited.

Is managing a new generation of Asian workforce so different from what it used to be a decade ago?

Many Asian leaders are competent when it comes to executing their functional or technical roles. Most leaders have admitted that their biggest challenge is dealing with the people issues. How does one motivate uncommitted staff? How do you manage conflict between two employees who do not get along? How does one provide constructive feedback to an under-performer? What about that smart alec who behaves as if he knows everything?

These are people-related issues that managers face on a daily basis. The assumption by organizations is that managers should know how to handle them. Consequently, they are not provided the necessary leadership soft-skills training, resulting in organizations performing below-par.

Today, millennials make up over a third of the workforce. They are a lot more educated, tech-savvy and socially connected to the global economy. The concept of "sharing-economy" or uberization and mobile apps are the in-thing. Flexible work arrangement, corporate social responsibility and frequent performance conversation are the new preference or norm for employee value proposition. Notwithstanding, let's not forget the baby boomers who are remaining employed longer. They have the loyalty and work-centric mindset that conflicts with the millennial work ethics. How does a twenty-first century leader handle these generation gaps and expectations in their team?

Leading High-Performance Team is a fable that takes place in a small and medium-sized business setting. It entails its technological and economic challenges that this traditional business owner is facing. Add to the fact that his millennial daughter who recently joined him is struggling to adapt culturally in helping the company stay relevant. Obviously, the mindset and leadership styles among the management team had to change first. They needed to adapt to the changing environment so as to overcome their adversity in work and in life.

The characteristics of a high-performance team are gradually uncovered as the story unfolds to enable you to grasp the concept and importance. We hope that you will gather as much practical tips as possible so as to make your leadership journey a fruitful and enriching one.

1.

IT'S TIME

It was past ten o'clock on Thursday evening in early January for John. His phone has been beeping with text messages for the last hour. They were messages from his staff.

"What's the urgent communications meeting tomorrow morning at 9am about?" Joe asked.

"Is something happening tomorrow that I should be concerned about?" came Sally's message.

John decided not to answer the text messages for once. After all, he had been in a meeting with Jane, the Asia Pacific HR Director the whole day. He was exhausted and he needed some time to plan his speech the next morning. As he sat down, he reflected back on the ten years he had with the company as the General Manager. Indeed, there were many challenges but there were also many wonderful moments. He felt a sense of satisfaction.

The next morning, John was in his office before 7.30 A.M. He could not sleep the whole night so he decided to go to the office early. Jane came by his office at 8 A.M. and they went through some last-minute discussion.

At 9 A.M. sharp, John walked into the conference room. Surprisingly everyone was on time which was rare. There were just over fifty people from all the various departments cramped inside the conference room with some standing at the back. John could sense the worried look on some of their faces even though they gave a smile when he looked around.

John took a minute to compose himself before he began. "Good morning, everyone. First of all, I would like to thank everyone for being here even though we called for this meeting only yesterday. I know that some of you had to change your customers' appointment. I really appreciate that"

"Let me get down to the reason for this meeting. I will try and keep this meeting to an hour," John said as the room fell into silence. "As all of you are aware, we have been going through challenging times over the last two years. Many of our manufacturing customers have moved to northern Asia, and the global manufacturing industry has undergone lots of changes."

"Over the last three months, the management team in Asia Pacific has been in discussion with the corporate headquarters in US on the plans for our South East Asia operations here in Singapore. We went through many iterations and justifications for this year's plan. The ultimate decision unfortunately is to shrink down the operation in Singapore." John paused. There was a shocked and concerned look on everyone's faces.

"The decision is to cut down fifty percent of the headcount here, including the Malaysia, Thailand and Indonesia operations." John paused again. "I know it's a drastic cut but we still managed to justify a skeleton workforce to service the existing customer base. I will be going through the list of people who will be affected by this layoff. It will be with immediate effect. The good news is that we managed to secure one month's retrenchment benefit for every year that you have worked in the company."

John composed himself again. "I would also like to let you know that I will be leaving the company as part of this cut." The room erupted with shock as they heard this news.

"Who's going to run this place?" asked Jason, the sales account manager.

"The functional head will now report directly to the Asia Pacific functional directors," John said.

John proceeded to name the list of people who were affected by the cut and fielded questions from the group. John ended the meeting by saying, "It has been a fruitful journey working with all of you. We have become a great team, just like a family. We have definitely had lots of fun working together all these years, and I hope we can continue to keep in touch with each other as we start a new chapter in our lives."

John announcing the list

There were a lot of mixed emotions as the meeting ended. Some were in tears, hugging each other while a couple left the room immediately without much words. Those who were retrenched were asked to see Jane, the HR Director. John stayed behind in the room to answer some questions from the remaining crowd. It has been the most heart-wrenching meeting that he had to conduct in his entire corporate life.

"Could this be my last?" he thought.

2.

COFFEE CHAT

It was 3 P.M. on Sunday and John was sitting at Starbucks café in Raffles City Shopping Mall. He was waiting for Victor Ong who had just texted him to say that he was running about ten minutes late. He had bumped into Victor the week before Christmas while shopping with his wife, May. He hadn't seen Victor for almost twenty years and they had arranged to meet up for coffee.

John reflected back on the first time he met Victor. He had just graduated from the local university, and Victor was his supervisor in his first job. Even though Victor had only a diploma qualification, John respected him greatly. Victor was a very smart and conscientious supervisor. He was like a mentor to John and showed him the ropes of being a good engineer. Victor eventually left the company to set up his own business. John moved on to other roles in other companies and was fortunate to move up the corporate ladder to where he is now.

Victor appeared shortly and apologized to John for being late.

"I just came from our family lunch, and my second

daughter, Rachel, told us she is expecting our first grandchild in June!" said Victor with a smile.

"Congratulations, that's wonderful news," replied John.

"How have you been? You still look the same after all these years," said Victor.

"It has been great! Although my company recently underwent some restructuring. We had to let go about half of our workforce here. I just made the announcement to them on Friday. It was tough." John continued. "I also put up my name as part of the restructuring to reduce the overall cost and to save a few more headcounts. It took a while to convince the HQ, but eventually they did agree to let me go as long as I help them transition properly over the next one month."

"So sorry to hear that," answered Victor.

"Well, I'm actually looking forward to this. I've been thinking and discussing with my wife for a while now. I've always wanted to come out to start my own business, just like you, but never had the courage. This a good opportunity to do that," John answered confidently.

"Have you decided on what you are going to do?" asked Victor curiously.

"Not yet. I've considered a couple of options but I'll probably spend more time reviewing the options once I've settled the handover in my company," John said. "Enough of me, how have you been Victor?"

"It has been a roller coaster ride for me. As you probably know, I started the business distributing cash registers to retailers over twenty-five years ago. Cash register has progressed to POS systems over the last two decades. It was good business back then. Now everyone is talking about e-commerce, mobile tablets and even mobile payments. The whole industry is changing and competition is getting tougher. Besides, the retail industry is undergoing a downturn at this moment. So, it has been challenging lately." Victor said as he sipped his latte.

"What are your thoughts moving forward?" John asked.

"Definitely, I'm not sitting still if that's what you are asking me," Victor answered. "I've acquired a local software company eighteen months ago. It is a small team of twelve engineers. They specialize in e-commerce and customer relationship management software. They have also developed an interesting mobile payment system which I thought would complement our existing customer base. I believe the technology can help our traditional retail and F&B customers transition to the mobile platform. At the same time, we can help them move some of their business online using our integrated e-commerce technology." Victor paused for a short moment. "I've also asked my eldest daughter, Tricia, to join my company a year ago. She had graduated with a Computer Science degree from the University of California, Berkeley and has worked for three startups in Silicon Valley for about eight years. After she received her MBA, I managed to convince her to come back to Singapore to help me in our business development efforts."

"Wow, you are so lucky," said John. "I remember her back then when she was probably about five years old when you used to bring her to the office. She was so cute and adorable."

"Well, she's 32 this year." replied Victor. "It hasn't been easy for her, or myself for that matter, over the past year. I can see her frustration working with the existing team. We have had a number of big arguments over our future expansion plans. She has a lot of great ideas. Perhaps she is very aggressive and used to the fast pace in the startups back in Silicon Valley. So, coming to a traditionally run company like mine might be something that she's not comfortable with." Victor continued, "There are times when we don't speak for a few days after a major argument."

John could sense the sadness and regret in Victor's voice. He asked Victor with a concerned tone: "What would you have liked to see instead?"

Victor paused for a minute before replying. "You know I'm going to be sixty next year. I do want to take a backseat and spend more time with my wife and with my future grandchild. I've been considering for a while about who could possibly take over the business. I was hoping that Tricia could be the one. But I'm not too sure if she is ready and whether she would be interested. I know she is still young and it may take many years before the rest of the staff, who are much older than her, would accept her as the boss. I was hoping that she could take over in the next two years, but it doesn't seem to be likely. Besides, the argument that has been going on is not too healthy. I wish the situation would be much better."

John thought for a while before asking "Suppose that you are able to get to where you want to be in two years. What would it take for you to achieve that?"

Victor took another sip of his latte as he pondered over that question. "Perhaps I could be more open to Tricia's ideas and let her have more say in the decision. After all, she is a lot more tech-savvy than I am. I could also talk to some of the management team and ask them to support her. Or maybe find someone to guide her along the way."

Victor suddenly looked at John as if a light bulb just went off. "John, why don't you come and work for me as my General Manager. I know that you may have other plans. Perhaps not long term, could be a two to three years' contract. Your leadership experience in the corporate world will be of tremendous help to us. Tricia can learn a lot from you. Besides, she would probably be more receptive to someone external than to her own dad. We could use your expertise to streamline our operations especially with the new company that we acquired. What do you think?"

John was taken by surprise. Here he was meeting Victor for the first time after almost twenty years and suddenly this offer! He was wondering why Victor trusted him to offer him the GM position. He said "This is really unexpected. I really appreciate the trust that you have in me. I would need to think over this and discuss with May."

"Yes, please think over it seriously. You know, in the short time that we have been here, I can see that you are still the same authentic and trustworthy guy whom I knew. I've always had a feeling that you will be successful in your career. It will be great to have the chance to work with you again," said Victor excitedly.

Both John and Victor continued to chat about the old times and some of their ex-colleagues. John promised to get back to Victor within two weeks on his decision. He still had to travel to the other offices to make the restructuring announcement and to do the necessary transitions.

As John drove home after the coffee chat, he thought about the offer from Victor. He had been thinking about setting up his own management consulting and coaching business. John had attended a coaching certification course five years ago. At that time, he had considered the possibility of becoming a business or leadership coach. "How will Victor's offer affect my decision to set up my own coaching business?" John thought to himself as he arrived home.

3.

THE TAXI RIDE

John was waiting in the taxi queue at Changi Airport. It was about 7 P.M. on a Friday evening, and he had just returned from a business trip to Penang. It has been a hectic few days in his Malaysian office as he helped smoothen out the transition. The whole transition has been going much better than he had expected. As he entered the taxi, he thought about his coffee chat with Victor two weeks earlier. He decided to give Victor a call.

"Hey John. How have you been? Been waiting for your call." John could hear Victor's excited voice over his mobile.

"I'm doing well. I just returned from a business trip to Penang and I thought I would give you a call," replied John. I've been thinking over what we discussed the other day. I've also had a lengthy discussion with May on this matter. Your offer really sounds very attractive. Can I offer you a counter proposal?" asked John.

"Please do," replied Victor immediately.

"I would still like to kick off my own coaching business. It's something that I've been thinking for a while. What I would like to propose is that I could work for you on a part-time basis, perhaps twice a week to see how I can help you and Tricia for the next one year. This will allow some time for me to explore my own business. Perhaps I could come in every Tuesday and Friday. Does that sound ok for you?" asked John.

After a moment of silence, Victor spoke "Sure! That will work too. I've also been thinking since our last conversation on the areas that you can help me. Besides Tricia, I would also like you to meet up with all my management team. Perhaps you can coach them on areas for improvement. I can share more with you on the issues that we are facing when we meet up. When can you start?"

"I should be able to complete all the transition with my company by the end of this month. The first week of February is the Chinese New Year holiday. How about the second week of February?" asked John.

"Yes, second week of February will be perfect. Our company will be closed for the first week of February anyway. I can't wait to tell Tricia about our arrangement," replied Victor.

They chatted over the phone for a short while more. As the taxi pulled up towards John's apartment, he bid farewell to Victor and wished him and his family an early Happy Chinese New Year.

As John waited for the lift to his apartment, he thought to himself, "That went pretty well." He felt an excitement in him as his plan and vision started to form in his mind. By working part-time with Victor, he still has a small income while he builds up his coaching business. Besides, Victor had been a great mentor to him in his early years. This would be a great opportunity for John to repay him.

The experience that he could gain coaching Victor's company would definitely add-on to his credential.

He cannot wait to share the good news with May.

4.

INTELLIGENT RETAIL
SOLUTION

As John walked out of the lift on the eighth floor of a flatted factory building, he saw the big company signage "Intelligent Retail Solution (IRS) Pte Ltd". This was his first day at Victor's company and he was feeling excited yet nervous. He opened the glass door to the reception area. There was no one at the reception counter, so he decided to wait for a while.

It must have been about five minutes before a matured and stern looking lady, probably in her late fifties, came out to the reception area. "Yes?" she asked in a serious tone.

"I am here to see Victor. Please let him know it is John Chen," replied John.

"Take a seat," replied the lady in her monotonous voice as she picked up the phone to call Victor.

"She must be having a bad day," thought John as he took a seat on the couch.

It was about ten minutes later before Victor appeared.

He apologized to John for the wait as he was on the phone with a client. As they walked to his office, Victor told John that he just got off the phone with the boss of an important client. He was complaining about the problems that have been unresolved for over a month, and that it has impacted their business.

Victor showed John into his office. As John took a seat across Victor's desk, Victor said, "John, if you don't mind, could you give me a couple of minutes while I call my service guy to look into this matter."

"Sure, please take your time. I fully understand the importance of this matter," replied John as he looked around the office. It was about half the size of John's previous company office. There were piles of documents all over Victor's table as well as on the chair next to where John was sitting. He also noticed some boxes containing old POS equipment lying at the corner of the office. John thought to himself, "Is this what it is like working in an SME?"

"Sorry" said Victor as he hung up the phone. "I have told Paul, my Technical Service Manager to solve the problem by this week regardless of what it takes! Sometimes when you don't give them a deadline, they will take their time. The engineers don't seem to understand the importance of pleasing the customers."

"Anyway, enough of that," said Victor. "John, thank you for coming in and helping me on a part-time basis. I know we are not paying you much but we can definitely tap on your expertise to see how we can grow our business. I have also told Tricia that you will be coming in today. You can meet up with her after this."

"Great!" replied John. "Victor, perhaps you can share with me more about your company and your vision for the company."

As Victor started sharing, John took out his notebook and jotted down some of the key points.

Halfway through the meeting, they were interrupted by a knock on the door. At the door was a petite young-looking lady dressed in white T-shirt and black jeans, smiling at them.

"John" said Victor. "Let me introduce Tricia to you," as she walked in.

"Tricia, so nice to finally meet you. I've heard so much about you from your dad. You have really grown up," said John as he shook her hand. "Not too sure if you remember me, but I still remember you as this cute little girl many years ago."

"Ha Ha" Tricia laughed. "Not really," replied Tricia. "But dad did tell me about you coming on board during our recent Chinese New Year reunion dinner. I look forward to working with you."

"I have to apologize," continued Tricia. "I know we are supposed to meet up today but one of my colleague, Paul, just asked me to go for an urgent meeting with a client together with his engineer to resolve some issues. It will likely take the whole day. I hope we can postpone our meeting?"

"Oh, yes. I heard about the issue earlier," replied John with a smile. "How about this Friday at 10 A.M. instead?"

"Sure, this Friday is good. I am really sorry for the last-minute change. See you then." Tricia then bid farewell to them.

Both Victor and John continued with their discussion.

"What are some of your key challenges?" asked John.

Victor paused for a while and said "People." He continued. "You know, John, sometimes I joke with my friends. SME does not stand for small and medium enterprise, it's Super Man Entrepreneur! I feel that I have to be a superman, doing everything, being everywhere."

"Don't get me wrong. I have good people. The management team and, in general, the rest of the employees are hard-working folks. However, they are always waiting for my instructions. If I don't jump on them, things don't move. I have to follow up on everything. I wish they can be more independent. Otherwise I don't think this company can grow fast enough. For example, I have been asking Eric, who is my Sales Director, and his team to work with Gary, who came from VSI, the company that we acquired. Eric and his team need to understand the new technology that we have so that they can upsell our new solution to the existing customers. It has been eighteen months and we have hardly penetrated into our existing customers with the new technology. It's frustrating," Victor exclaimed.

"What might be the reasons behind this situation?" asked John.

"I don't know. That is where I was hoping to tap on your expert opinion," replied Victor.

"Well, I would definitely like to meet up with your management team to learn more from them. But based on your gut feel, what could be the underlying reasons why things are not going according to what you expect?" asked John.

Victor paused for a short moment. "Maybe the sales team do not understand the new technology well enough and are afraid to sell to the customers," said Victor. "Or maybe there is a working relationship issue between Eric and Gary because of their age difference. Eric is in his mid-fifties and Gary is 38 this year."

"These are potentially two very good observations that you have brought up. It's very useful information to know and I will find out more when I meet up with them," John continued. "I'm curious, Victor, you have shared some exciting vision and goals earlier with me. Have you shared that with your staff?"

"Well, I've mentioned bits and pieces to Tricia and a couple of the senior management team. But not to everyone. I don't want to scare everyone with this big picture when we are not there yet, in case some of them are not comfortable with the new direction," said Victor.

"I understand your concern. Can I share my thoughts on this?" asked John.

"Sure, of course," said Victor.

"Over the last twenty-five years working in the MNCs, I find that it is very important that the CEO of the company share his vision and goals. This could be a three to five years' vision with clear objectives of what the company plans to do. Even when you are twenty thousand miles away from the HQ, every one of us down to the receptionist is aware of where the company is going. As a regional operation here, we are fully aligned with the corporate goals and we build and execute our business plans accordingly without much intervention from the CEO. Each division, each department, understands its own roles and responsibility. Because of this clarity, the execution of each division is aligned to and contributes towards the organization's vision," John continued. "When you shared where you would like the company to be in five years, I was really excited. I'm very sure the rest of your staff would be too."

"Interesting, I never thought of it that way," said Victor. "Perhaps, I should share my vision and goals at the management meeting next week. I could get their inputs before I share it with the rest of the company. I'll put together some presentation materials and run through with you on Friday. I'll arrange the meeting next Tuesday so that you can join in as well."

"That will be perfect," said John excitedly.

Both Victor and John went for a simple noodle lunch at the canteen opposite their office building. When they came back, Victor showed John around the office and introduced him to the management team and some of the employees.

At the end of the office visit, Victor brought John to the meeting room. "The meeting room is empty if you would like to use for the day. I apologize we don't have a spare desk or room for you. I will check with Serene, my HR/Finance manager when she is back from her leave tomorrow to see if she can find a space for you on Friday."

"No worries. I'll use this meeting room for a while before I call it a day," said John.

As John sat down in the meeting room, he started to reflect on his meeting with Victor and the people whom he has met that day. He wrote down a few details in his notebook. He decided to draw the organizational chart that Victor had mentioned for his easy reference.

John had also indicated their age on the chart based on what he had gathered from Victor. He had a feeling that their age differences may have played a part in how they deal with each other. It is an issue he has observed over the years working with many of his Asian colleagues.

Victor Ong
Managing Director
(Age 59) - 53 staff

Tricia Ong
Business Dev Director
(32)

Serene Pereira
Finance/HR Manager
(40) - 3 staff

Gary Tay
Software Director
(38) - 11 staff

Eric Lee
Sales Director
(55) - 8 staff

Paul Thomas
Tech Services Manager
(48) - 12 staff

AK Lim
Marketing Manager
(39) - 2 staff

Othman Din
Operations Manager
(59) - 10 staff

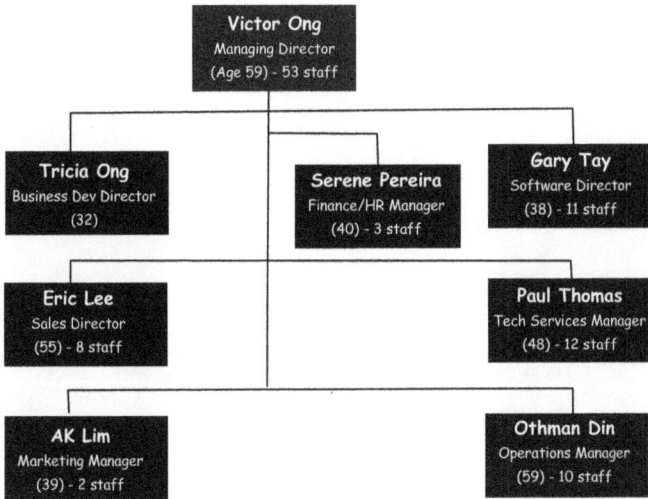

Organizational Chart of Intelligent Retail Solution Management Team

As it was approaching 5 P.M., John decided to call it a day so that he can avoid the traffic jam. He knew the traffic in that industrial estate will build up very soon. After all, he could not remember a day in his last twenty-five years in the corporate world that he had left before the sun set. He smiled as he walked towards his car with the evening sun still shining brightly in the west.

5.

TRICIA

At 10 A.M. sharp on Friday, Tricia knocked on the door of the meeting room where John was working. She was dressed in her usual white T-shirt and black jeans, though this time she had a black jacket over her T-shirt as she entered the room.

"Good Morning, Uncle John," said Tricia.

"Hi, Tricia. Please call me John," replied John. "I have worked in US multinationals for a long time, and we call each other by the first name regardless of our age. I know I've met Uncle Thomas and Aunty Teresa from the operations department the other day. It's right to address them by 'Uncle' and 'Aunty' as a show of respect given their age. But for me just call me John," smiled John.

"Sure, John," said Tricia sheepishly.

"It's amazing how time flies. Tell me more about yourself, Tricia," said John.

Tricia shared with John about her work at Silicon Valley and the wonderful time she had working for the three startup companies. She talked about how every employee was so motivated at their workplace, coming up with great ideas every day. The leaders there were not very much older than most of the employees and they were very receptive and supportive of their views and ideas. Everyone was putting in fifteen to eighteen hours shift. And they still had time to have fun together.

Even though she was working long hours, she managed to pursue her MBA part-time at Stanford Graduate School of Business. Shortly after her graduation, her dad asked her to come back to Singapore. Her mum had just taken ill, and he wanted Tricia to be back to help him with his business, so that he can spend more time with her mum.

"Oh, so sorry to hear about your mum. Your dad did not mention about her. How is your mum doing?" asked John.

"She's better now. She had some form of rare blood disorder. It took many months for the doctor to diagnose the actual cause. Initially, she was bedridden and in pain most of the time. Now, she is taking a special medication and she is now able to move around more freely," replied Tricia.

"That's good to hear," said John. "Tricia, ever since you joined the company, how has that been for you?"

Tricia pondered over the question and said, "It was a culture shock initially. The way things are run here and the people's attitude is quite different from Silicon Valley. It took me at least six months to get used to this."

"I see," John continued, "Do you regret coming back to Singapore?"

John noticed the long silence and the slight watery eyes before she said, "You know I'm the eldest daughter in the family. Even though things were looking bright for me in my last company, I felt the obligation to come back and help the family. After all, my parents gave me the opportunity to study aboard. I should at least do my duty. My younger sister who is a tax consultant with one of the big four auditing firms was not too keen to leave her cushy job. Besides, she married last year and she is now expecting her first kid."

"It has not been easy working alongside my dad to be honest. He can be quite demanding at times and he has his own way of doing things. Maybe he expects a lot from me and I haven't been able to meet his expectation," said Tricia.

Tricia in deep thought

"Do you know what his expectation is?" asked John.

"Not really. He never spoke about it." Tricia continued, "I guess he wants me to be like him. For now, I will try and help wherever I can. I am technically quite savvy. So, when there is a problem, I will work with the team to get it resolved."

"Do you think by continuing this way, it will help you and the company?" asked John.

"Probably not. I was hoping to hear your advice on this. I guess that's the reason why my dad decided to hire you as our part-time consultant," smiled Tricia.

"Well, 'consultant' might be too big a word. I would rather call myself a coach. My role is to listen to your situation, and ask questions to help you discover the solution for yourself. You are a Berkeley graduate with an MBA from Stanford. You have the knowledge and expertise to come up with the right solution. All you need is for someone to help you be more aware of your situation and to discover the possibilities for yourself."

"Ok" said Tricia with a puzzled tone.

"Shall we take a ten minutes' break before continuing?" asked John as they strolled out of the meeting room.

6.

BUILDING TRUST

"Tricia, earlier you mentioned that the people's attitude here is quite different from Silicon Valley. Can you tell me more about it?" asked John as they continued their conversation.

"Back then, everyone was so self-motivated. They work independently making sure they deliver the results that they promised. Sure, we challenge and debate with each other in meetings, voicing our opinions. But at the end of the day, we will agree on something and everyone goes about doing their part." Tricia continued, "Here, most of them do not want to say much during the discussion. Whether they agree with my suggestion, I don't really know. Sometimes the work gets done, other times no. I'm not too sure if that's because I'm the boss's daughter. Some just do it because they feel obliged to. Also, many of my colleagues are much older than me, as you can probably see. I don't know what goes through their mind when they have to listen to someone much younger than them."

John listened actively as she continued to share some

of her situations and frustrations. He could sense her disappointment and predicament. Yet, at the same time, she is also sensitive to the fact that she is the daughter of the business owner and did not want to assert her authority.

Tricia also shared with John on an upcoming government tender. This project is part of the government's initiative towards a cashless society. She believes that with the technology acquired from VSI and her knowledge on Blockchain technology that she acquired in Silicon Valley, they would be able to meet the tender requirements. However, she seems to be facing a roadblock from Gary to allocate the required resources for the project.

"What can you do differently for them to be more open during discussions and be more receptive to your suggestions?" asked John.

"I guess I would have to encourage them to speak up. I should be more patient and listen to their suggestions, rather than sharing my ideas first," said Tricia.

"Or maybe I have to get to know them better so that they become more comfortable working with me," continued Tricia. "Perhaps I should buy them lunch more often," she said with a chuckle.

"These are great ways indeed," said John. "One of the challenges when someone new comes on board a company is the ability to gain the trust of the existing team members. And it's likely to be even more challenging if this is a family member."

"When you build trust with someone, you need to remember there are two types of trust. Do you know what they are?" John asked.

"Good and bad trust?" replied Tricia jokingly.

"The first type of trust is *Competency Trust*" said John.

"And what I mean by competency trust is the trust that you build based on your credentials or abilities. For example, you have a string of impressive educational qualification plus your Silicon Valley experience. I'm very sure the rest of your colleagues admire your abilities and are more likely to listen to you when you offer your technical opinions!" John noticed Tricia nodding her head as he continued.

"The second type of trust which is a lot harder to earn is *Character Trust*. This comes from your personal character strengths of courage and justice.

'Have you treated them fairly? Do they believe that you will have their backs when things go wrong? Have you demonstrated that you have kept to your words? Did you walk the talk? Did you take responsibility for the failure or did you point finger at someone else?' These are questions that comes to mind when we talk about character trust. This will take time to build." said John.

"I see. So, I need to be patient to build up the character trust?" said Tricia simply.

"Yes, unfortunately. But I can share one way you can quickly build trust. By acknowledging and validating someone!" said John.

"How often have we noticed someone doing a good job, but we kept quiet about it, letting it pass? We should take the opportunity to complement the person for his or her actions, and acknowledge how that action has helped or impacted others or the business positively. That will make the person feel good. When others feel that you appreciate them, they will begin to trust you more," said John.

"However, the validation has to be genuine. It has to be authentic, coming from your heart. People will eventually know when you are insincere. When that happens, you will lose all the trust with them." John continued, "In our culture, many of us are not comfortable complementing someone else. We grew up in a culture where you only feedback on areas of improvement. Our parents, teachers and bosses tell us: 'it's not good enough...you can do better.' Because of that, we are not showing enough appreciation to many of our employees. Besides, if they feel appreciated, they will become more motivated!"

"That's awesome, John," said Tricia. "I should do more validation going forward. And, of course, it has to be authentic," she smiled as she said "In fact, I think I'll do that right after this. I must complement Sanjeev, who is the engineer who went with me to see the client on Tuesday. He worked late into the night to debug the issue and managed to resolve the problem the next day."

"One more thing, Tricia," added John. "When you validate him, complement him on his actions and effort rather than his abilities like intelligence or how smart he is. Let him know how his actions and effort resulted in a positive effect for the customers."

"Why did you say not to complement him on his abilities?" asked Tricia.

"Well, that would probably take some time to explain.

In short, you want to encourage the right behavior by complementing on his action and effort. We can leave it for another day to discuss further since it is lunch time." said John as they wrap up the session.

Tricia thanked John for his time listening and coaching her. It was a very useful session and she would love to have more of such sessions. John agreed and told her that he would rope her in at the appropriate time when he meets up with the rest of the management team. He believes she can learn a lot just by being in the session. After all, she is a fast learner.

In a Nutshell

For effective relationship, you will need to build both **competency trust** as well as **character trust**. Competency trust can be easily demonstrated through your abilities, credentials and experience. Character trust takes time to build.

7.

ALIGNED GOALS AND VISION

It was the second week with IRS for John. He was in the usual and only meeting room of the company. But this time around, he was with the whole management team. Victor had called for the meeting to share his vision for the company. He began the meeting by telling the team that he envisioned IRS to be the industry leader in mobile payment platform for the ASEAN region. No longer will they be confined to the traditional retail and F&B industry. He believes that they can provide a seamless payment application across all industries.

He set the goal for the company to achieve $30 million dollars within the next five years, up from the current $20 million annual revenue. As he said that, John noticed some concerned look from the team.

"How do we plan to achieve that?" interrupted Eric.

"Well, if we can win the $15 million government contract this year, it will be a step closer. It is a three-year project to equip the relevant government agencies with a unified payment system. This will add a good revenue stream for us each year. On top of that, once we can get the endorsement from the government, we will be able to leverage on the publicity to penetrate into the other industries with our technology," said Victor confidently.

"But are we ready to compete with the big boys who have the latest and greatest technology?" asked AK, the marketing manager.

"Today, we have a sizeable market share of the retail and F&B market. We have a good track record and understanding of the local businesses. Our VSI technology has already been implemented in a few of the government agencies and we are getting positive feedback. We certainly can have a shot at this," replied Victor.

John decided to interject: "Not to mention, I understand from Tricia that she has a lot of experience with chainblock technology that will be useful for this project."

"Blockchain Technology" corrected Tricia, laughing.

"Oh yes. Blockchain," continued John. "Tricia is the expert in this and she will be sharing the technology with all of you later."

John recalled his session with Victor last week when he was going through the presentation materials with him. John had suggested to Victor on letting Tricia present the technology pitch to the team. He felt that it will help build up some competency trust with the management team.

Victor shared his second goal of expanding into the Indo-China region, in particular Vietnam, Myanmar and Cambodia as a start. These are the fastest growing economy especially in the traditional retail and F&B sector. Given their expertise in these industries, he believes it will be a good starting point. He plans to set up operations in each of these countries within the next two years.

There was a sense of excitement in the room as Victor elaborated further. John was happy that Victor had taken his suggestion on sharing his goals and vision with the team. Now his leadership team has a clearer picture of where the company is heading towards.

"The third key goal that I would like to set is on people development," Victor said. "It is an area that we have neglected all these years. As we grow our business, we need to upskill our people and to attract new talent into our company. I have brought John in not just to help us in our business operations. I believe he will be able to assist us tremendously in showing us how we can develop our people, given his experience in the corporate world. And when I say people development, it is not just for the employees, it will also include the management team. I've asked John to meet up with each of you to explore areas where he can help you and your team to perform better. Please use this opportunity to tap on his expertise."

Shortly after, Tricia took over to present the details of the blockchain technology and how it can benefit the customers and the company. She was very passionate and comfortable in explaining how the company can integrate all the various technology into a robust and seamless platform. She showed a lot of confidence in addressing the technical questions from Gary and Paul. In fact, John noticed the "proud father" look on Victor's face during the presentation. As expected, Victor did not praise her at the end of the presentation.

John decided to chip in. "I don't know how all of you feel about Tricia's presentation. But personally, I am really excited about how this technology can help the company to propel forward. I feel pretty confident that if all of you can come together to build on this, you can beat the big boys!"

"Yes, let's do it!" boomed Din, the operations manager in his usual jovial tone.

This was followed by some laughter, smile and nods of agreement from the rest of the team.

"Could I ask the team how you can make this happen?" asked John.

There was a moment of silence before Gary spoke. "Perhaps we can form a team consisting of Tricia, myself, a few of my engineers and maybe a few from the sales or services team."

"Like a cross-functional team or a special project team," reiterated John. "That's an excellent idea!"

The team proceeded to discuss the list of potential people to be included in the special project team. Victor also took the opportunity to discuss with the team on the plans and the people who will be responsible in meeting the goals that he has set out. The meeting turned out to be much better than what John had expected. He thought to himself, "Sharing the company vision and getting all the organization to align to the goals is really powerful, much more than what I have envisaged."

John took out his notebook and wrote down on a clean page. At the top of the page, he wrote: 'Characteristics of High-Performance Team'. Below the title, he wrote '1. Aligned Goals & Vision (Victor)' to remind him of Victor's session. He also wrote down '2. Building Trust (Tricia)' as he recalled his session with Tricia.

He may be on to something, as he reflected on the notes.

In a Nutshell

Sharing the organizational **vision** *and getting every team member to* **align** *to the organization* **goals** *is essential in building a high-performance team.*

8.

MANAGING MILLENNIALS

It was early March morning. John was having coffee with Eric at the canteen opposite their building. The only meeting room in the company was occupied, so John suggested to have a coffee session with Eric instead. Eric was in his neatly pressed white shirt, blue tie and black pants. He was well groomed and energetic; no one would have guessed he was in his mid-fifties.

Eric was sharing his life story with John. He was the first sales representative that Victor hired over twenty years ago. He had always appreciated the sales skills that Victor had taught him over the years. Now that he is the sales director of the company, he feels the obligation to impart his skills to his team. He has a team of eight sales representatives, six of whom have been with him for more than ten years. They are in their forties and fifties now. Recently, he hired two new sales representatives in their late twenties. He felt that his older team members are struggling to keep up with the advances in technology. They are used to selling the traditional POS system.

"Now that e-commerce and mobile technology are the

in-thing, the company feels that we should hire younger and more tech-savvy people," laments Eric. "The two younger sales reps have computer science degree and have worked in sales for two to three other companies already!"

"Nowadays, the millennials seem to job hop all the time," continued Eric. "And they do not seem to listen to what I tell them unlike my older staff. To the extent that sometimes I have to scold them 'bodoh'."

John understood 'bodoh' meant stupid in Malay and had noticed Eric using some of these words intermittently in his past conversation. After all, Eric is a Peranakan. A Peranakan is a straits-born Chinese with mixed Chinese and Malay heritage. A Peranakan man can be very expressive and detailed in nature, John remembered.

"What positives do the two younger members bring to your team?" asked John as he sipped his coffee.

"Well, as I mentioned earlier, they understand all these new technologies much better than most of us," said Eric. "I've seen some of their proposals to the customers and I have to admit they are quite interesting, something which I would not have thought of."

"I'm curious what you mean when you say their proposal is quite interesting," asked John.

"I guess the right word would be creative. Somehow, they can craft out a proposal that exceeds the customer's expectation. Yet it is something that our technical team can deliver." Eric continued, "For the rest of my older staff, they seem to be proposing the standard old offerings that they have been doing for years."

"That's one of the reasons why I'm considering assigning Jessica, the new sales rep, to work in the special project team that we discussed the other day. She can be the main point of sales contact for the government authority, National Fintech Agency (NFA), that is putting up the tender in July. She has worked on government tenders in her previous job so she is familiar with the process. I believe she is resourceful enough to convince NFA to consider our proposal. Besides, I think she has the ability to network around and connect socially with the youthful tender committee," said Eric jokingly.

"But other than that, it's a chore managing these two millennials. They don't seem to follow what I tell them to do: to submit the weekly sales forecast, fill up the customer profile, log in their activity reports and many more. It is like they can only do one thing at a time, unlike our generation where we can multi-task," laments Eric.

"Eric, it's interesting that you said 'managing the two millennials'," said John. "You know, the last thing millennials want is to be 'managed'! I have had the opportunity to work with many millennials in my previous job. One of the great things about them which you have mentioned is that they are creative and resourceful. Initially we had the same challenge managing them. Over the years, we have learnt to coach them instead!"

"Before we can coach them, as leaders, we have to change our mindset. I've shared with many of my previous leaders on the three mindset shifts," continued John.

"Firstly, we have to change our attitude from an Advisor to a *Facilitator*. The fact is the world is changing so fast. Our experiences and the problems that we have encountered in the past are likely to be different from today's. We may not be able to fully comprehend the situation and possible scenarios that our employees are facing both internally and externally. If we try to provide solutions based on our past encounters, they may not be relevant to today's context. So as leaders, our role is to facilitate and enable them to *develop their own customized solution* that works for them."

"Secondly, we have to believe that they are *creative and resourceful*, just like what you have said about Jessica. When we believe in them, they will feel motived. No matter what challenge they encounter, they will have that self-belief and confidence to come up with the most creative solution."

"Thirdly, as leaders, we have to *focus on their strengths* and not their weaknesses. When we explore strengths, successes and abilities, they will be more motivated as compared to hearing their weaknesses. While we shouldn't ignore their weaknesses, it should not be emphasized during coaching. By leveraging on their strengths, we are able to help them move forward towards the goal immediately. It helps to build up their confidence."

"Hmmm. In other words, I should avoid sounding like a broken record. Telling them they haven't done this and that and calling them 'bodoh'," said Eric.

"It is really interesting what you just said on the three mindset shifts. I should seriously put more thoughts into that," added Eric.

"Yes, think over it. Even better, try it out and see what happens," said John.

"Eric, you mentioned the possibility of including Jessica as part of the special project team. Should we rope-in Tricia in to discuss further?" asked John.

"Sure. Let me check with Tricia on her schedule and I'll keep you informed," said Eric.

"How has it been for you ever since Tricia started working with the company?" asked John.

"It's ok, John. I'm a very direct person. If you are asking me if Tricia takes over her father as the boss, would I work for her?" said Eric smiling. "You know, John. I'm already 55. As long as I can continue to work, and if the company still wants me, it doesn't really matter who the boss is. I've known both Victor and, for that matter, Tricia for over twenty years. Victor always invites us to his house for Chinese New Year gathering. I've seen Tricia grown up over the years. To me, as long as my boss treats me with respect, I'll respect them back. Even though Tricia is young and aggressive, she is a person who respects others. Personally, I think most of the managers here would not have any issue working for Tricia when the day comes. Besides, she is technically so savvy, and the company probably needs someone like her to lead. Although I can't say the same about Gary."

"Oh, why do you say that?" asked John with a curious tone.

"Well, when Victor bought Gary's company back then, Gary probably had the idea that he would have a much bigger role to play in the company. Now that Tricia is on board, I don't know how Gary feels. Anyway, that's just my opinion, don't quote me," said Eric.

"Thanks for sharing, Eric," replied John as both of them headed back to the office.

In a Nutshell

*To effectively coach others, especially the millennials, we have to **change our mindset**. As leaders, our role is to **facilitate** and **enable** them to **develop their own customized solution** that works for them.*

9.

EMPOWERMENT

"John, you know, I've been thinking over the three mindset shifts you mentioned last week," said Eric. "I tried to practise it with Jessica."

"Three mindset shifts?" asked Tricia inquisitively as the three of them sat down for the meeting.

"That's what old dogs like me have to learn and re-learn new tricks to handle young people like you!" said Eric as he turned to Tricia.

"Well, the three mindset shifts are:

- Be a Facilitator, not an Advisor
- Believe that all of you are creative and resourceful
- Focus on your strengths, rather than weaknesses

Is that correct, John?" asked Eric.

"Absolutely right!" replied John enthusiastically. "Tell me more about your story with Jessica."

"Well, I spoke to Jessica right after our meeting that day. I told her that I admire her resourcefulness and the creative proposals that she had put up previously. I've asked her if she would be keen to join the special project team, so that we can leverage on her strengths. She would have to work closely with Tricia and the rest of the team and provide her with creative juice from a sales perspective. She was very enthusiastic about it. In fact, I notice she seems more motivated the last couple of days. Maybe she is happy that I am not breathing down her neck every day," said Eric sarcastically.

Both Tricia and John laughed. The three of them started their discussion on the role that Jessica can play in the team. They also discussed the background of the client NFA and their expectations. The tender is less than four months away and they would definitely have to craft out a good strategy and engagement plan with NFA.

As they were wrapping up the discussion, John turned to Eric: "Eric, the other day, you mentioned that your older staff are struggling with some of the new technology. How do you think we can help them?" John asked as he remembered his conversation with Victor on this issue.

"Yeah, I know. I'm supposed to arrange with Gary for him to update the team on the new technology and how to sell to our customers. My guys are so busy running around every day chasing numbers, attending to clients' issues, filling up activity reports, forecasting etc. It is so hard to find the time for them to sit down and learn," laments Eric.

"I can empathize that time could be a factor. What other reasons could be a deterrent for them?" asked John.

Eric pondered for a moment and said, "it might be the fear of learning new technology. They may not have the confidence to talk to their customers for fear that they do not have all the answers."

"They will always come to me whenever there are

problems related to the POS systems or to ask me for help with their proposal. Now, they know I'm as blur as them when it comes to the new stuff. I feel so helpless at times when I don't have the answers for them. Sometimes, I have to 'kawan kawan' with Paul to get help," said Eric.

John understood 'kawan kawan' meant 'to make friends' as he thought over what Eric had just said.

"You know, Eric, it's interesting what you just said. As leaders, we don't always have to have all the answers. Our role is to facilitate our team to be skilled to solve their own problems. They need to take responsibility for their own actions, even for their own learnings. The key message here is *empowerment*," said John.

Empowerment requires mindset shift

"We can help facilitate their learning process. At the end of the day, they need to be motivated themselves to learn. Remember the three mindset shifts that you mentioned earlier. When you empower them to take their own actions, they will be more accountable for themselves. It's all about *shared leadership*." John continued, "It is also important to leverage on the strengths of the whole company. Your sales team does not have to be an expert with all the technical jargons. They just need to know how to position the technology and open doors with the clients. They can tap onto the expertise of Paul and Gary's team when the time comes."

Tricia had been listening intently to what John said and

decided to chip in. "Eric, perhaps I can put together a set of sales deck which your team can use to help open doors with the clients. I can go through with your sales team on how to pitch to the client. I believe I have a good idea of the sales team's technical capabilities, so I'll tailor it within their means. We should also set up a meeting with Paul and Gary to work on the engagement process whenever your team requires help. Would that be useful?"

"That sounds fantastic!" Eric replied excitedly as he left for a client meeting.

Tricia thanked John for the session and told him about the good learnings she has received. That reminded John. He quickly flipped his notebook to the "Characteristics of High-Performance Team" page and wrote down "3. Empowerment (Eric)" as he explained to Tricia what he has been doing.

In a Nutshell

Shared leadership is about *empowering* your team members to be *accountable* for their own actions and learnings.

10.

CREATING AWARENESS

It was the middle of the day on Friday as John stepped off the elevator on the second floor of Copthorne Waterfront Hotel. It was full of people mingling around looking at the exhibits.

"It must be coffee break," John thought, as he walked around looking for the IRS booth. This was an industry seminar on "Digitalization" for the SME customers and IRS had set up a booth to showcase their technology. John was there to meet up with AK Lim, who is the marketing manager.

As the crowd started to return to the ballroom for the final part of the day's presentation, AK told John, "Let's grab a coffee and find a quiet corner to talk."

"How is the show coming along?" asked John.

"Oh, it's very good! There were lots of enquiries and interest on our offerings. The participants from today's seminar seem genuinely more interested compared to previous events," said AK enthusiastically.

"Hopefully, we can generate some good leads out of this," continued AK. "John, my sincere apologies for postponing our last two meetings. I was so caught up preparing for this event. And since we are having this event today, I thought it is a good idea to invite you here to see what we are doing."

"Looking at the crowd surrounding IRS booth earlier, it definitely looks promising. Thank you for inviting me here. It is really an eye opener for me," said John.

AK shared with John that he had spent fifteen years working for a local telecommunications company in various marketing role before coming out as an entrepreneur to start his own retail business. Within the first two years, he had opened up five stores. Unfortunately, he expanded too fast, and the retail industry took a downturn in the last three years. He took that painful decision to close his business a year ago. He was a client of IRS POS systems and the company was looking for a marketing manager at that point in time. He ended up joining the company to spearhead the marketing and branding efforts for IRS. He was very passionate sharing his marketing strategy. He loves to keep himself updated on the latest trends and strategies from articles and books on innovative companies like Amazon, Google, Apple and Facebook.

However, he felt that IRS was too slow in adapting to the change. Victor and the management team were not that receptive to his branding strategy and marketing plans that he had developed.

John remembered his conversation with Victor that some of the marketing promotions that the team came up with did not yield any results. He had also gathered feedback from others that AK was not listening to their real needs. He seems to have his own views on the kind of promotion the company should have.

"AK, I really admire your passion and the creativity that you have put into the strategies. I am curious to know what might be the reasons why the management team is not receptive to your proposals?" asked John.

"They are not visionary enough unlike many of the leading technology companies out there. They are too slow to change and not thinking out of the box," AK replied confidently.

"I see. Are there other reasons?" asked John.

AK thought for a moment and said "Perhaps the company is not ready yet, both from a people as well as from a technology standpoint."

John remained silent and waited for AK to continue.

"Maybe the market is not ready for some of the creative marketing promotions that we did?"

"And how would you be able to verify these?" John asked with a sincere look.

AK pondered over the question for a minute. "Perhaps

I can check with the sales team to get their inputs. After all, they are on the ground most of the time. I'll also need to gather more feedback from the rest of the management team to understand their concerns."

"That is very good insight!" said John. "How do you plan to get that done?"

"Well, we are planning to meet up with the sales team after we compile the leads from today's event. I can take the opportunity to get their views and ideas on the type of marketing promotion that we can run. As for the management team, I would probably have to find time to meet up with some of them individually to understand their concerns and to get their inputs," AK paused momentarily.

"Thanks John for making me aware of my situation. I know I can be quite stubborn and impatient at times. Just focusing on coming out with the latest marketing strategy without listening to what's really needed. I would probably have to learn more from you. You have been so patient listening to me for the last forty minutes," said AK.

"No problem. I am so glad I can be of help. Indeed, as leaders, we have to be good listeners. Otherwise, everyone will be going about doing their own things based on what they view as important. There will be a lack of coherency in the whole organization.

"AK, if you would like, I am having a session with Tricia on Tuesday morning at 10 A.M. I can spend some time to share with both you on what you should be listening for as a leader. Would you like to join us? No obligations of course," said John humbly.

"Yes, that will be wonderful. Really appreciate your advice. I look forward to catching up with both of you on Tuesday," replied AK as he headed back to his exhibition booth.

In a Nutshell

*Before any **behavioral change** can happen, you will need to **create that awareness** with the person.*

11.

ACTIVE LISTENING

"Tricia, how is your special project team meeting coming along?" asked John as they waited for AK. AK had just messaged them that he will be fifteen minutes late.

"It's ok, although it could be better," replied Tricia.

John could detect a sense of disappointment in Tricia's tone and body language.

"Would you like to elaborate further?" asked John curiously.

Tricia told John they had their first meeting the day before. The meeting started well initially as they discussed the objectives of the team. As the meeting progressed, she felt that some of the members were not as open and supportive when it came to their roles and responsibility. There were also a couple of occasions where she had disagreements with Gary on the team's approach.

"What do you think could be the reasons for the disagreement?" asked John.

After a short pause, Tricia said, "Personally, I think he wants to take control of the meeting. I believe he wants to demonstrate that he is the leader of the project. I could be wrong, but that's my gut feel."

"Well, even though I wasn't at the meeting, I am inclined to believe you. A lot of times, your gut feel tends to be correct," said John smiling.

"I have a question, Tricia. Is it important for you to lead the project?" asked John.

"You know, John, all I want is for the company to succeed. I don't need to have the glory, to be known as the leader. All I care is to do the right thing for the company," replied Tricia.

"Spoken like a true leader," said John smiling again. "When is your next meeting? Perhaps I can sit in as an observer."

"We are meeting again next Friday at 2 P.M. It will be great if you can join in," said Tricia as AK walked into the room apologetically.

"AK, great that you are able to join us. I wanted to use this session to share my thoughts on how we communicate as leaders. Communication is a two-way process. Unfortunately, leaders tend to forget and end up just having one-way communication. Can you guess which way is missing?" asked John.

"Listening," both Tricia and AK replied in unison.

"Absolutely!" continued John. "There are *four levels of listening:*

- Ignoring, which is lowest level. That's when we are totally switched off.

- Selective Listening, where the leader has already made up his or her mind, and just waiting for the opportunity to speak.

- Attentive Listening, where one is listening to the *content* of what is said.

- *Active Listening*, which is when one is listening for both the content and context as well as for the unsaid.

To be a good leader, one has to be listening at the active level."

"I have to admit I'm probably between level one and two," said AK sheepishly.

"Do you know why it's important to listen actively?" asked John.

"To make the other person feel understood which in turns help to build the relationship and trust," replied Tricia.

"Yes, and when you have the trust, the other person will be more willing to express their thoughts and ideas. They may even share the underlying reasons that caused the problems which, as leaders, we may not always get to see or hear."

"Also, as leaders, when you are able to listen actively, you will be able to better understand your staff situation. This will facilitate *asking the right questions* to help them discover the solution for themselves," said John.

"It sounds logical. But it seems so difficult to listen at that level," said AK.

"Yes, it takes practice. AK, what are the reasons that are preventing you from listening actively?" asked John.

AK thought for a while and replied "It could be my past experiences that are influencing me. For example, if certain marketing promotions have worked well in my previous job, I will try and replicate them here. So, I stopped listening to my team and customers."

"Could it also be because we tend to be judgmental? Because if we have a preconceived idea of the person, we may not be as open to them," said Tricia.

John knew Tricia was referring to the fact that she has

lesser experience when compared to the team. Moreover, she is also the daughter of the founder.

"Both of you are correct!" John continued. "When we are not mindful of the situation, we can be distracted from listening actively. So, it is important to be mindful, open and curious. Put aside past experiences or preconceived ideas. *Be fully present* when you are listening to the other party.

"Let me give you an analogy. Both of you can probably relate to this. Suppose you want to install a software application onto your computer, and your hard disk is full. Are you able to do that?"

"Obviously you can't, right?" said John as both Tricia and AK shook their head. "So, what can you do?" asked John.

"Delete some unwanted files to free up the space," said Tricia. "Or we could just forget about installing the software application," replied AK jokingly.

"Precisely!" John said excitedly. "When our minds are full of thoughts, preconceived ideas, beliefs or judgements, nothing can go in. We are not listening to what the other party is saying. It is like the hard disk that is full of old photos, videos, documents and applications. We need to let go of all the old stuff that are no longer useful."

"But John, in the case of the computer, we can simply delete files. How do we delete the thoughts from our minds?" asked AK curiously.

"Good question, AK," smiled John. "Just like the computer that needs regular maintenance like disk cleanup for optimal performance and to receive new data, our mind requires similar treatment. That is where the *practice of mindfulness* comes in. If you are able to take time off regularly to meditate or engage in mindfulness practice, you will realize that you can learn to silent your mind – free it from the load of thoughts.

"It does not necessarily mean practising mindfulness all the time in that full lotus sitting posture that you often see in yoga or meditation retreat. It could be as simple as mindful eating. The next time when you eat your meal, slow down, chew and enjoy every bite. Learn to savor the taste of every ingredient in the food. The idea of being mindful is being here in the present moment, being conscious of what is happening right here, without the external distraction of, for example, your mobile devices or the inner chatter that goes on in your head. You can exercise mindfulness even when you are walking, driving or just talking to another person.

"What is important is to be fully in the present moment, do one thing at a time and enjoy every moment. When you practise regularly, you will find that you will become more mindful. When you become more mindful, you will in fact be more productive and happier with your life."

"That is really interesting," said AK. "I should give it a try."

"Now, let's get back to the subject of listening," continued John.

In a Nutshell

To **listen actively**, one has to be **fully present**, **open** and **curious**, putting aside any preconceived ideas or judgment.

12.

WAYS OF LISTENING

"This may sound coincidental, but do you know that besides the four levels of listening, there are four ways of listening?" said John as he went to the white board and started to draw four quadrants.

On the top left quadrant, he wrote down 'Listen With'.

"What do we use to listen?" John continued. "With our senses, of course; our ears, eyes and our heart. We also need to listen with a positive mindset. Free from all the barriers that we discussed earlier. We need to be open-minded, curious and empathetic."

"Both of you are probably familiar with the traditional Chinese character of listen, 'Ting'," John wrote on the board.

"As you can see, there are characters of our senses; the ears, eyes, and heart." John continued, "We use our ears to listen to what the other person is saying. Our eyes can listen and see the non-verbal cues, such as the body language. We also need to listen with our heart. In other words, listen with empathy, putting yourself in the other person's shoes."

Ears (Verbal cues)

King (Respect Open-mind)

Ten (Fully)

Eyes (Non-verbal cues)

One (Solely)

Heart (Empathy)

Chinese Character of Listen "Ting"

"There are also the characters of 'ten' and 'one' which tell us that we need to give our undivided attention to the person in front of us, just like the respect that we give to a 'king', which is the last character. We need to listen with an open and positive mindset."

John proceeded to write on the top right quadrant 'Listen By.' "Anyone?" he asked.

"Using technology?" said AK jokingly.

"That's an interesting one," quipped John. "But it is really about how we show that we are listening. You can demonstrate using positive body language such as leaning forward, head nodding or smiling. Just like the two of you are doing right now. These are called non-verbal signs. We can also demonstrate through verbal signs such as asking clarifying questions, validating and acknowledging."

"It sounds so simple, yet most of us have taken listening for granted," said Tricia. "Let me guess, the next one is Listen To?"

"You are absolutely right" said John as he wrote 'Listen To' on the bottom right quadrant. "What do we listen to?"

"Gossips and secrets?" joked AK again. Everyone laughed.

"Well almost," said John. "We listen to the content of what the person is saying, like what you just said. It includes the story, issues, ideas and feelings. On top of that, we also listen to the context, in other words, the bigger picture. How the story is related to the bigger issue?"

"For example," continued John, "when I was a young manager, there was a brilliant engineer who came to me one day to inform me that he wanted to resign. The reason he gave was that he was taking a teaching job so that he can spend more time with his newly married wife. Without fully understanding the situation, I told him he had a promising career ahead of him, with the potential to be the regional head of engineering. I could not understand why he would give all that up. Moreover, he seems to be enjoying his job and getting all the recognition. The discussion to convince him to stay was in vain.

"It was about a week later that another colleague came to give me the full picture. Apparently, his wife had this phobia of his frequent flying. It was a painful decision for him to leave the company, but that was the only way he could allay her fears. After knowing that, we convinced him to stay by reassuring him that we will minimize his travel. Instead, he could support our clients remotely through the use of technology, and we could send other engineers to service them when required. After all, the other engineers love to travel. In the end, it turned out to be a win-win situation for everyone.

"So, it is really important not just to listen to the content. We need to understand how this relates to the whole story."

Finally, at the bottom left quadrant, John scribbled 'Listen For' as he looked at Tricia and AK to response.

"No idea?" asked John.

Below 'Listen To', he wrote down 'Obvious' and finally 'Unsaid' under 'Listen For'.

"This is the most difficult part of listening, to listen for the unsaid. It is not explicitly said by the person. However, if you listen closely, you can uncover a person's beliefs, assumptions, strengths, values and personality," said John.

"Wow, you probably need to be a Jedi to be able to do that!" joked AK.

"Actually, all of us have the ability to do that. It is part of our natural instinct. It is a matter of whether you take the trouble to listen for them. When you are more mindful, you will be surprised at how powerful your listening capabilities can be," said John.

"Practise with the next person whom you talk to. Try and listen for that person's character strength. For example, did he or she demonstrate strengths such as creativity, leadership, honesty or humility in the conversation? When you as a leader can identify the strengths of your team, you can take the opportunity to validate them to build the trust, and to leverage on their strengths."

Both Tricia and AK nodded their heads in agreement. This was a good learning session for them.

In a Nutshell

*When we listen, we need to listen with all our **senses** and with an **open mindset**. Listen to what is **obvious** as well as for the **unsaid**.*

13.

NO TIME

"Xiao Long Bao!" shouted the waitress as she placed the dumpling dish on the table. "Have you tried this before?" asked John as he opened the cover of the steaming bamboo basket.

"Yes, I had this with my family in this restaurant a couple of times before," replied Paul Thomas.

John was having lunch with Paul. It had been difficult to find time to meet up with Paul due to his packed schedule. John decided to invite Paul for lunch instead. Both Paul and John had briefly worked together in their first MNC job under Victor. Paul was originally from Bangalore in India. The company had posted him to Singapore for a six-month project assignment. After a short stint in the Bangalore office, he applied for a job with a local company in Singapore and eventually moved here. He has since settled down locally with his wife and two kids.

Victor asked Paul to join him about fifteen years ago when the company started to move from cash register to POS systems. He was one of the first few engineers hired by Victor, and he was promoted to Technical Service Manager about five years ago.

Paul was the same unassuming guy that John had known when they first met. He was technically very talented with very positive work ethics. All the engineers look up to him.

"So sorry, John. I know you have been trying to schedule a meeting with me for the last month. I have been tied up with two major customers to install our POS systems for their chain of stores. We encountered some issues and it took a while to resolve," said Paul.

"No problem. I fully understand," replied John. "Are things getting better?"

Paul laughed. "Well, it has been pretty much the same all these years. There is usually a pipeline of new installations. Existing clients continue to call every day with all kinds of technical issues. Our hotline never stops ringing."

"Is that because of the nature of this business?" asked John inquisitively.

"I guess so. The users from the retail, food and beverage industry are not technically savvy as you can imagine. Sometimes the issue could be as simple as a loose printer cable. But my engineer can spend an hour troubleshooting over the phone before discovering the real problem.

"Today we have more than two thousand clients on active maintenance. And I have only twelve engineers to handle new installations as well as support customers. Not to mention that we also provide 24×7 priority support to some clients. That is why I have to be personally involved in some of the major installations," said Paul.

"Wow, I can't imagine how busy you and your team can get!" continued John. "Have you considered how you would handle the demand now that the company is moving into newer technologies besides the POS systems?"

"Not really," said Paul "I have been so busy. I simply have no time to plan. Every time I start to look into it, my engineers will come to me with issues. My time will be spent helping them to solve the problem."

"It is interesting you mention that your engineers keep coming to you for help to solve their problems," said John.

"Well, I guess they treat me like a guru. It is the fastest way for them to resolve issues, especially when those demanding clients want immediate attention," said Paul.

"Paul, I do understand the need to resolve clients' issues quickly. But if your engineers keep coming to you for solutions, where do you find the time as a leader to evaluate, plan, develop and grow your organization?" asked John.

Paul pondered for a while and said, "I guess you have a point. I have been managing this way for the last five years. I never really thought of it otherwise.

"But what can I do? I simply can't tell my engineers not to come to me for help, right? As a manager, that is my value to them."

"On the contrary, Paul," replied John, "as a manager, you *manage systems and processes,* not people. As a leader, you *lead teams! Leading team is about enabling and developing people.* The real value that you can provide is to develop their capabilities so that they can solve the problems themselves, not by providing solutions for them. Otherwise, they will never grow.

"When your team is independent, you will have the time to review and enhance your systems and processes. With the improvement, it will enable your people to be more productive and efficient," said John.

"That is an interesting way of looking at it. But what

would you suggest I can do to develop my people? Give them more training?" asked Paul.

"Not necessary. It does not have to be training. You can consider changing your approach," continued John. "The next time they approach you for help, instead of giving them the solution, why don't you coach them?"

"Well, I have been coaching them all these years. I have been very patient and nice to them, listening to their problems," said Paul.

"Yes, that is a common misconception for many managers," said John smiling. "They think that they are coaching, but it is not the case.

"Paul, I know you have a customer meeting after this. I have my usual session with Tricia next Tuesday morning at 10 A.M. Would you be available to join us? I can share with you more about what coaching is."

After a minute of silence, Paul said, "Yes, why not. I guess I don't want to spend the rest of my life going through the same thing every day. Sure, I will make myself available on Tuesday. Thanks, John." They then called for the bill.

In a Nutshell

As a manager, you **manage systems and processes**, not people. As a leader, you **lead teams!** Leading team is about **enabling and developing people.**

14.

COACHING

"Anyone of you can tell me the difference between coaching and mentoring?" asked John as he started his session with Tricia and Paul.

"Sounds almost the same to me," quipped Paul.

"I think mentoring is when someone more senior teaches a younger person, while coaching can be done by someone young or old, just like a sports coach," said Tricia.

"Not really," said John. "One of our roles as leaders is to develop people. To do that, we'll need to understand what are the helping skills we should use for the different situations.

"We are familiar with *teaching* or *training*. It is a skill technical people like yourself are very conversant in. You teach someone when they lack the knowledge or knowhow to perform a task. In short, you are *imparting knowledge* to the other person."

John added, "For example, Paul, when you hire a new engineer, you will probably start training him or her on how to operate the POS system. But your training will not be able to cover all the possible scenarios that can go wrong. Along the way, the engineer may encounter a problem that he cannot solve. Of course, the easiest way is to tell him the solution if you know the answer. In this case, you are teaching him.

"Imagine the permutations of problems out there, not just technical issues but also human related issues. You want to avoid the situation where your engineers keep coming back to you for the solution.

Teaching

"Another helping skill that most leaders are good at is mentoring. Many leaders love to share their past experiences, to the extent that some team members may find their boss over egoistic!" John laughed. "*Mentoring* is about *sharing one's wisdom* to *facilitate the mentee to move forward*. The mentor is someone who has walked a similar path and is able to share his or her experience and wisdom.

Mentoring

"I am quite sure you have had employees coming to you to complaint about a difficult colleague. Perhaps that colleague is so self-centered and unwilling to do his or her part for the team."

Both Tricia and Paul nodded their head as John continued.

"Chances are that you may have encountered such people in the past. You may share that experience and advise on how to handle such a situation. It may not always work of course, as each situation or person is different. But essentially, you are mentoring your employee."

"I guess I have been teaching and mentoring my staff all these years. Then what is coaching?" asked Paul.

Coaching

"That is a good question. Most leaders think that they have been coaching their people through a combination of teaching and mentoring. This is a misconception. In coaching, we help the other person or coachee to be *self-aware* and to *facilitate self-discovery*. Coaching is a process where we use a range of communication skills such as active listening and powerful questioning. We help the coachee look at various perspective in order for them to achieve their goals. We avoid giving our opinions, views or suggestions."

"It is probably a lot more difficult than it sounds, right?" asked Tricia.

"Let me share with you a story," continued John. "Some years ago, one of my managers hired a project engineer from Taiwan. He was technically very experienced with all the right credentials to manage a project that we had just won. Within two months, there was a lot of tension between this project engineer and my manager. The engineer was constantly late in his report submission. He skipped many of the internal meetings, offering excuses about attending to the client's needs. My manager scolded him and they got into a heated argument.

"I called for a meeting with the engineer. Initially he was very defensive. It was only in the second meeting, after I have assured him of my open and non-judgmental approach that he started to open up. He told me that his reason for coming to Singapore is because his wife wanted their only son to have an education here. He was a supervisor managing a team of engineers back in Taiwan. He gave up a promising career because of the family.

"I asked him what the consequences would be if he continued with his current behaviors. He became aware that it wasn't going to help his family nor improve his work situation. He openly admitted that he can be very stubborn. He hated being monitored or supervised all the time. I can empathize with him, given his previous role as a supervisor. Eventually, between the manager and the engineer, we worked out a process and approach that was agreeable to all parties. His behavior improved and he became more motivated. He completed the project in two years with high commendation from the client. Subsequently, he left to start his own business and he is doing very well.

"The fact is that we tend to jump to conclusion and label these employees as bad. If we take the effort to be *open and curious*, to *create awareness* in them, we can help them self-discover and achieve their goals."

In a Nutshell

*Coaching is a process of helping the other person or coachee to be **self-aware** and to **facilitate self-discovery**.*

15.

ASKING THE RIGHT QUESTION

"John, earlier you mentioned about asking powerful questions. How do we know what is the right question to ask? Is there a manual of powerful questions?" asked Paul laughingly.

"Like your technical manuals of FAQs?" smiled John.

"Well, there are compilations of coaching questions out there. But that would be too mechanical and unnatural to ask all those questions!" John continued.

"First of all, a useful rule of thumb is to ask *open-ended questions*. I guess you know what open-ended questions typically starts with?" John paused to look curiously at them for the answers.

"5 Wives and 1 Husband," joked Paul. "What, When, Where, Who, Why and How?"

"Yes! For example, Paul, if I were to ask you 'What would it take for you to develop the plans for the new company vision?' versus 'Have you completed the plans for the new vision?'

"Which question is more likely to get you into actions?" asked John.

"The first one of course," replied Paul.

"Precisely. The second question is closed-ended. It would simply be a yes or no answer. If it is a no, it is unlikely to spur you into action. Unless there was a stick behind that question," smiled John.

"The first question forces you to contemplate before replying. At the minimum, it would get you to think about when and what are the actions to take to achieve the goal. Also, when you verbalize the actions, you are more likely to act on it. It might even get you to think about the reason for not working on it. You may also question the importance of the task."

"Gee, I never thought there was so much difference and impact from the way we ask questions!" exclaimed Paul.

"So does that mean we should always be asking open-ended questions? Isn't it kind of awkward and unnatural?" asked Tricia.

"That is a good point. Typically, as a leader coach, we should ask more open-ended questions, about eighty percent of the time. It is alright to ask closed-ended questions to elicit confirmation or decision. But try to minimize the usage of closed-ended questions.

"You also brought up a good point, Tricia, about feeling awkward asking all those open-ended questions. It might feel interrogative when you start shooting the questions. Just like how it feels being questioned at the police station!" said John.

"To make it less interrogative, listen and be silent after asking a question. You can also ask clarifying questions or paraphrase to demonstrate that you are listening actively. Validate or acknowledge the other person wherever possible. Then ask the next question. In this way, the other person will feel less intimidated.

"For many of the Asian managers, asking open-ended questions may not come naturally. Most of us have been conditioned from young, by our parents, teachers and by our Asian supervisors, in our working life. Our parents are always asking us, 'Have you eaten your lunch? Have you taken your shower?' Teachers tend to ask the students 'Did you submit the homework? Is this statement true or false?'

"Our school systems in the past have trained us to regurgitate the right answers during examinations. You are rewarded for the correct answers and punished for the wrong ones. The students do not question the teachers on the theories presented. Neither are they asked for their thoughts and opinions on various subjects.

"Similarly, when your employees encounter a challenge, they will come to you expecting an answer. Start by asking open-ended questions to get them to think and reflect for themselves. Initially, it might seem strange to them. Let them know that you are coaching and developing them. The important thing as leaders is to facilitate and help them come up with the various options. The chosen option should be their choice. The ultimate goal is to enable the employees to design their own actions. They will be more accountable as compared to being told what to do," added John.

"Over time, they may even learn to self-coach, asking the questions to think through for themselves. They may come to you for opinions on the various options, which is fine. The key here is that they become more independent and responsible for themselves. You will then have more time to strategize and plan for the organization," said John.

In a Nutshell

*In order to develop your employees, ask more **open-ended questions** to help them to **think** and **reflect** so that they can come up with their own **customized solutions**.*

16.

INTENT OF QUESTION

"Is it just as simple as asking open-ended question?" asked Tricia.

"Great question, Tricia. I was coming to that. The second rule of thumb is to understand the *intent* of your question. What is the *purpose* of asking the question?

"Many times, leaders ask questions for their own benefit. Just to get an update or gather more information about the situation. Personally, I've seen many managers in the past whose only interest is to gather as much information from their team. They can then update their bosses and look smart. This does not help the employees in any way.

"When we ask questions, we need to remember that the purpose is to help our employees think, reflect and make the appropriate decision. If you know that the employee is lacking in confidence, you can ask questions to evoke his or her confidence. For example, there was a sales manager in my last company who was struggling to meet his sales target for a particular year. He was facing some challenges closing a major deal because of competition. This was a deal that would make or break his whole year's target. At one stage, we could see that he was demoralized. Our competitors were achieving much better results during the client's benchmarking evaluation. I decided to take him aside for a chat. I reminded him of his past successes as a sales manager in our region. Some questions that I asked were:

'What was that one achievement that you were proud of?'

'What were three positive qualities that you demonstrated?'

'What positives did the client say about you?'

"It helped him to believe in himself. More significantly, it helped to trigger off ideas that he had not thought of previously. And you would probably have guessed the outcome. He ended the year as the top sales manager in the Asia Pacific region for closing that major deal," said John.

"What I have just highlighted is leveraging on *Success Principle* to *evoke confidence*," continued John. "I could also have used *Anticipatory Principle* to help my sales manager *expand his possibilities*. In other words, I could get him to imagine achieving the goal. The positive image and emotion will motivate him to move forward. Some questions that one can use include:

'Suppose that you are able to win the deal, what would happen?'

'What if the benchmark result was not as critical to the client's decision? What difference would that make?'"

"John, when you ask questions based on these principles, it is not that difficult to come up with the right questions," said Tricia confidently. "In fact, you have given me an idea on how I can approach the special project team in our subsequent meetings. I can get them to paint a vision of winning the tender. And ask how each of them will feel in terms of the achievement. How it help build their credentials? Hopefully, they would not be as calculative when it comes to roles and responsibilities."

"That is a brilliant idea, Tricia!" John exclaimed. "So happy to see the speed at which you are applying the principles. Another useful principle that you can use is the *Constructionist Principle*. All of us have our own personal beliefs, values, habits and perspective. We are influenced and conditioned by who and what others say or do. When it is said or done many times, it can become the truth in our mind.

"Let me share a story of an old monk living in a monastery. Someone in the village had given the monastery a kitten. Initially, when the monks were doing their afternoon chanting, the kitten would play around the hall and disturb the old monk. So the old monk decided to let the kitten out of the hall every day before he starts the chanting.

"Soon after, the old monk passed away, and the senior monks would do the same every afternoon: let the kitten, which by now had grown into a cat, out of the hall before chanting. The senior monks eventually passed away, and the junior monks would continue the tradition of letting the cat out.

"Eventually, the cat passed away. So, guess what the monks did. They went to the village to ask for a new cat so that they can continue the tradition. They had come to believe that letting the cat out before the chanting session is part of the whole ritual. They have never questioned the reason behind it in the first place," said John.

"Very interesting story indeed," Paul replied.

"Yes, all of us will fall into the same trap. That is why as leaders, we need to *challenge our employees on their assumptions and beliefs*. If we see that our employees' beliefs are preventing them from performing at their best, we can ask questions like:

'What are some assumptions that you have here?'

'How useful is it for you to hold on to this belief?'

'If these assumptions were no longer present, how would you do it differently?'

"Sometimes, you may not get the appropriate response immediately. Personal views, perspectives and especially beliefs are deeply rooted matters. It takes time for one to change his or her perspective," John added.

"So, in summary, the two rules of thumb are?" John look inquisitively at the two of them.

"Ask open-ended questions," replied Paul.

"Know the intent of the questions and leverage on the various principles," said Tricia.

"Well done," continued John. "When you are able to take these into consideration, you are asking powerful questions. You are facilitating their thinking, reflection and decision process. You are helping to expand their perspectives and views of their situation. In short, you are developing them to be more independent, creative and resourceful."

*Asking powerful questions help to **evoke confidence**, **expand perspectives** and at times **challenge assumptions and self-limiting beliefs**.*

17.

BREAKFAST WITH GARY

It was an early Friday morning for John. He had decided to have a breakfast session with Gary at a nearby coffee shop before the second special project team meeting that afternoon.

While waiting for Gary, John pulled out his notebook and turned to his favorite page and wrote down "4.1 Communication – Active Listening (AK Lim), 4.2 Communication – Powerful Questioning (Paul)."

As he looked at his notebook, he noticed a pattern in the initials of the characteristics with that of the person he had spoken to. That was intriguing to John. Was this a coincidence? He wondered what characteristics would come out from Gary's discussion.

Gary appeared as John was putting his notebook away.

"My apologies for being late.

Charcteristics of High-Performance Team

1. Aligned Goals & Vision (Victor)

2. Building Trust (Tricia)

3. Empowerment (Eric)

4.1 Communication - Active Listening (AK Lim)

4.2 Communication - Powerful Questioning (Paul)

The traffic was a bit heavy this morning," said Gary as they both ordered their breakfast from the elderly tea auntie.

Gary shared with John that he was originally from Malaysia. He did very well in school and received an ASEAN scholarship to study in Singapore. He did his college and university in Singapore. With a first-class honors in Computer Science, he was immediately offered a software development job with a large multi-national company. After two years, he felt that the company did not recognize his abilities and he left to join a software startup. That startup lasted only three years before he and his ex-classmate started their own company, Vertex Systems Integration (VSI). In the initial years, they provided web design service, systems and network-integration for SMEs. Eventually, he and his partner had a fallout because of disagreement on the direction of the company. Gary wanted to focus on software development in the e-commerce, customer relationship management (CRM) and mobile payment applications. His partner, on the other hand, wanted to expand into systems and network integration. His partner eventually left to start up his own business.

About two years ago, he met Victor at a conference. Victor was very interested in the e-commerce and mobile payment technology that Gary had built. At that point in time, VSI was struggling to make inroads into the retail and F&B industry. With IRS's large customer base, and VSI's new technology, it was a marriage made in heaven. His team of eleven software developers joined IRS shortly after that.

"So, how has it been since you joined IRS?" John asked curiously.

"Well, I think it can be much better. We have one of

the best technology. It should have been well adopted by many of the clients by now," said Gary.

"What do you think is the issue?" John asked sincerely.

"I feel the sales team is not doing a good job. They don't have the capabilities to sell our technology to the clients. Selling the standard POS systems is very different from selling our customized software solution. In fact, I've asked Victor a couple of times to keep us as a separate division so that I can recruit my own sales team. But so far, he insisted that I should work with Eric to upskill his sales team. It has been quite frustrating indeed," exclaimed Gary.

"What could be the reasons Victor would want you to work with Eric's team instead of hiring your own sales team?" asked John.

"My guess is that he wants to keep the old team," replied Gary.

"I see, what other reasons could there be?" asked John.

Gary paused for a moment. "Maybe he still wants to focus in their existing area of expertise?"

"Any other possibilities?" John asked as he looked at Gary.

"Perhaps the sales team has the relationship with the clients. It will be easier for them to convince the clients to consider the new technology as compared to someone new trying to set foot into the account," said Gary, deep in thoughts.

"And if this was true, what would you do differently to work with the sales team and leverage on their good client relationship?" asked John.

Gary pondered over the question and said, "I guess if we can train the sales team on how to pitch the value of our new technology to the client, it can help to invoke the client's interest. When the time is right, they can rope me and my team in for a more in-depth discussion.

"In fact, I could even train two of my senior software developers to be pre-sales technical consultants. They will be the ones who can partner the sales team once the potential clients are identified," Gary said excitedly.

"That is a great idea, Gary," John said as the elderly tea auntie came by to clear away their empty plates.

18.

GROWTH MINDSET

"But, I'm still skeptical about the sales team capabilities?" Gary said as they continued their conversation.

"You know, Gary, all of us need to have the right mindset. And what I mean by the right mindset is what we call Growth Mindset. People with growth mindset *believe that capabilities can be developed.*

"Gary, you have been successful in your study and work life, especially having graduated with a first-class honors degree. Perhaps intelligence is something that came naturally to you. You probably did not have to work that hard to achieve your results, right?" Gary nodded his head as John continued.

"Because of that, you might perceive intelligence or one's ability as a fixed trait, something that you are born with. In other words, you are either a born musician like Mozart, an artist like Leonardo Da Vinci or a Usain Bolt, the fastest human on earth. Does that mean that Usain Bolt cannot be a good footballer if he wants to?

"A person with a growth mindset sees his or her abilities as something that can be cultivated. With the right attitude, that growth mindset person *sees challenges as a necessary part of learning.* He is *not afraid of taking risk or, for that matter, failure.*

"Take my eighty-year old mother for instance. She recently learnt how to use WhatsApp and Facebook so that she can keep in touch with her grandchildren living overseas. And the thing is that she has never touched a computer in her whole life. End of the day, it really boils down to one's motivation to learn!" exclaimed John.

Learning helps to grow our mind even as our body ages

"John, I see where you are coming from. I guess I have to be more open to the sales team. And not assume that they are not capable of learning new stuff," Gary said.

"Recently, I had a meeting with Eric and Tricia. We spoke about how to improve the capabilities of the sales team. In fact, Tricia had volunteered to put together some materials to help the team," John added.

"Oh, Tricia is going to do that?" asked Gary. John could sense something amiss with his tone.

"Perhaps, the two of you can sit down together to craft out the materials. After all, you know all the benefits of the technology," John said.

"No, that's fine. She should know what we have," replied Gary simply.

John thought for a moment as to how he should broach the subject of the special project team. He could sense some animosity coming from Gary whenever they talked about Tricia.

"Gary, I'm curious about your opinion on the blockchain technology that Tricia had mentioned to me previously. She was telling me about integrating that technology with what you guys have built to showcase for the upcoming government tender. What are your thoughts on it?" asked John.

"Personally, I'm not an expert in blockchain technology. From what I have heard, it is probably a lot of hype. There is still a long way to go as far as acceptance is concerned. Today, our technology can meet most of the capabilities that our clients require. I do not see the need for further development," Gary replied confidently.

"Well, I am certainly not a technology expert in this area either," said John laughingly as he continued. "I understand the importance of this NFA tender to the company. And the fact that the government is always interested to be in the forefront of everything especially the latest and greatest of technology. Do you think by going in with our current technology, we would stand a good chance?" John asked curiously.

After a minute of silence, Gary replied "Probably not."

John kept quiet for a moment before saying, "Gary, if you don't mind, could I share my observation from our conversation?"

"Sure, go ahead," said Gary.

"Please correct me if I am wrong. I get this feeling that you see Tricia as someone who is very smart with a good grasp of technology. You are probably concerned that if she is able to integrate all these technologies together, she might be seen as the technology leader in this company. Is my assumption accurate?" asked John.

There was a long silence before Gary said, "Maybe." The silence continued.

"Don't worry, Gary. You can think over it. I could be wrong," continued John. "I wanted to have a better understanding of your situation. Victor was a mentor to me when I first started my career. I have to thank him for where I am today. My goal is to help him grow this company. And the only way is to ensure everyone is aligned to the vision and work as a team. There are many external challenges that we face daily. The last thing we want is to create our own internal challenge.

"Like I have always told my team previously, we need to pick our battles. Using the military metaphor about winning the battle but losing the war, it is like achieving a minor victory that ultimately results in a larger defeat."

John thanked Gary for the meeting as they headed back to the office. John could see that Gary was deep in thoughts. He knew that it will not be easy for Gary to accept the current situation. After all, Gary had always been top of his class. He had built a startup successfully on his own. Now he is being confronted with a match in the form of the owner's daughter, Tricia, who could turn out to be as good as him or even better.

John wondered how the afternoon meeting is going to turn out.

In a Nutshell

A *growth mindset* person sees *challenges* as a necessary part of *learning*. He is *not afraid* of taking *risk* or for that matter, *failure*.

19.

CADENCE

After a quick lunch, John was back in the meeting room. He was excited to see how the special project team meeting would go. There were eight of them present, consisting of Tricia, Gary, Jessica from sales, three software developers from Gary's department, and two service engineers.

Tricia asked Gary if she could start off first. She painted the vision of the team and asked the team to imagine how it will feel like if they were to win the tender. This was the biggest high-profile project of its kind in Singapore and probably the whole of ASEAN region.

"If our technology is adopted throughout Singapore, how will this affect the millions of lives out there? Imagine the convenience that you will bring to everyone."

"If you win this project, what difference will that make to you personally?" asked Tricia.

The mood in the room certainly lit up after that as some of them came up with wild ideas of how they should celebrate if they win.

Tricia took the opportunity to start facilitating a

brainstorming session. They had to come up with ideas on how they can bring value to the client and to integrate the various technology. She was very open to the ideas thrown up and facilitated the session well. Everyone was fully energized and contributed to the discussion. All except Gary. John noticed he was quiet and deep in thoughts throughout the brainstorming session. The pendulum had swung to the other end, from what Tricia had shared with John in the first meeting. This was not a good sign and he had to figure a way to bring it to equilibrium.

As they were wrapping up the brainstorming session, John took the opportunity to interject.

"First of all, I want to congratulate all of you for your active participation. It is really great to see everyone embracing all the different ideas. That is a good trait of a high-performance team. We also have to be open and curious, trust and communicate well with each other. We need to have a growth mindset, to believe that we have the ability to develop ourselves and our technology if we put in the effort. Well done!"

John continued, "Gary, I was wondering if you have any other inputs for the team?" not knowing what will turn out from his question.

Gary was initially taken aback by the question. He said "Yes, I fully agree with what John has said. It was definitely a good session."

"Actually, I was thinking," Gary continued. "I hope John can continue to participate in our meetings whenever he can to provide his thoughts and views for the team. Likewise, I will continue to support the team especially from a technical development resource standpoint. Sometimes, I may not be able to be present for all the meetings due to the work commitment on some of the other projects. But I'm very confident Tricia will continue to be a good lead for the team. She has a lot of experience in this area and we should give her our full support!"

Everyone echoed in support at that point.

"Could I propose that we come up with a name for the team?" asked Gary.

"That will be awesome!" said Tricia excitedly.

Many names were thrown up during the brainstorming and eventually they agreed on "Cadence". All of them felt that it truly represented who they were and the rhythm that was building up towards success.

The meeting turned up to be much better than what John had anticipated. Tricia stayed back to talk to John.

"The meeting went pretty well!" Tricia said excitedly. "I'm surprised Gary asked me to lead the team. I was actually prepared to let him lead instead. I am curious what made him change his mind?"

John smiled and told Tricia in a teasing manner, "Maybe he knows you are smarter than him and you should be the ultimate leader for this team!"

Tricia laughed, "Well, the team has a lot of work ahead. We would definitely need to up our game!"

"Yes, indeed. Do keep Gary and myself updated on the Cadence meeting schedules. We will try our best to attend whenever we can. It is still important for you to work closely with Gary to get his support," John said.

"I will. Thanks John," replied Tricia as she left.

John took out his notebook. He wrote down "5. Growth Mindset (Gary)."

"It is really interesting how things are turning out!" John thought to himself.

20.

DEFENCE

"This is where we install and test the POS system when they first arrive," said Othman Din as he showed John around the operations department. It was already into April. John had spent the last two months with the other department leaders. Finally, here he was with Din showing him the heart of the operation.

"Thanks for showing me around the department and explaining the stuff that you guys do," said John as they settled down for a discussion.

"Din, I'll love to hear more about yourself," John said sincerely.

Din told John that he was a former schoolmate with Victor. They were in the school football team. Victor was the captain of their team then and Din was a defender. They had lost touch with each other after secondary school. It was during one of the school reunion that he met Victor again. Victor had already started IRS for about five years. He was looking for someone to help him with store operations and delivery and asked Din to join him. At that point in time, Din was working with a freight forwarding company and his practical experience in operations came in handy. He had always liked Victor for his leadership qualities. So here he was twenty years with IRS.

"That's an amazing story, Din," John said. "It is just like back in your school football team, where Victor is the captain of the company and you are holding the fort in the heart of defence!"

"Din, I'm curious to know how your team is doing?" asked John.

"Well, you probably know I am an easy-going guy. Most of my team are as old if not older than me. They have been with me for many years. I don't have to teach them much. They know exactly what needs to be done. Except for my two drivers. They don't stay with us for long. Most of them come and go. I guess that's the nature of the job. Other than that, everything else is cool!" said Din laughing.

"So, looks like you are in good shape!" asked John.

"Yes, you can say that. Of course, once in a while, we will call ourselves second class citizen," Din laughed as he said that. "You know, the sales and service team can be very last minute in their requests. They will throw us an urgent request towards the end of the day and expect us to ship out the systems the next morning. So my guys would have to work overtime just to meet their demands. But I'll always tell my guys to relax and not to be so worked up by this," Din said in a relaxed tone.

"Does this happen often? And do you know why it is always that urgent?" asked John inquisitively.

"For sure, it will always happen at the end of the month for the sales team. I guess they want to meet their monthly target, so they will push us to deliver the systems before the last day of the month!

"For the services team, I believe it is usually because the

system at the client's side suddenly fails and they need a replacement system immediately.

"Well, I see it as they are the strikers and midfielders who need to score the goals. As defenders, we just provide the support!" Din said jokingly.

They keep passing the ball to me!

"You are so wise indeed!" John added. "Din, based on your experience, what do you think can be done to improve the situation?"

Din thought for a moment. "I really don't think anything can be done. I have told the sales and services team many times not to give us last minute orders. But it does not seem to work! Maybe to them, they expect us to provide that support regardless.

"Moreover, they can be so messy at times. They will miss out or pass us wrong information because of the rush. When it goes to the finance department, you will hear Serene screaming at them. That is because they would have to regenerate the invoices multiple times."

"This is quite interesting. Regardless of whether you are in an organization or a football team, every team member has to understand how best to work with each other. You cannot always expect others to follow your idiosyncrasies," John continued. "I have an idea. Let me talk to Victor on this matter."

21.

SECOND CLASS CITIZEN

"Din, earlier you mentioned that sometimes you call your team second class citizen," said John as they continued their conversation.

"Yes, that is how most of us feel anyway. We seem to be getting the shorter end of the stick. I guess we have to accept that is the fact!" replied Din.

"Perhaps you may treat it like a joke. But when you say it often enough, your team may start to believe that is the case. When that happens, their behavior might be affected."

"Oh, I did not know it can be so serious," Din said.

"Let me share a story with you," continued John.

"Many years ago, there was an experiment carried out in one of the schools in the UK. At the end of a particular year-end examination, the results were not revealed. Only the principal and the consultants knew the results. What they did was to take the child who came in first in the exam and place him in the same class as the students that came in fourth, fifth, eighth, ninth and so on. The students who came in second, third, sixth, seventh and so on were placed in the other class. Basically, the students were split evenly between the two classes for the following year. They were assigned teachers of equal capabilities and given the same training resources. Everything was ensured to be as equal as possible. The only difference was one was called 'Class A', the other 'Class B'.

"The parents of Class A were very proud of their kids and they praised and rewarded them. Everyone had assumed that they were the smarter students. On the other hand, the parents of Class B scolded their kids for not working hard enough and took away their privileges. Even the teachers in Class B treated the students differently and taught them like Class B kids.

"Unsurprisingly but scarily, when that year-end examination results came out, the kids in Class A outperformed the kids in Class B. It appeared as if the students in Class A were from the top half of the class in the previous year. The other class had become Class B students, because they were treated like Class B kids and they believed that was the case."

"That is very interesting," said Din. "So that means I have to stop calling my team second class citizen!"

"Yes, when we start labelling someone in the negative sense, there is a high possibility that the person may turn out to be what they were labelled!" John said.

Both of them continued their conversation. John asked Din on what he thought about the company's new direction and how it would affect his team. Din agreed to put more thoughts into it and to arrange for further discussion with John at a later date.

*Research has shown the **negative impact** of **labelling** people (criticism or degradation).*

22

THE COACHING CONVERSATION

There was a knock on the door as a tired looking Tricia walked into the meeting room on a Tuesday morning. Tricia told John that the few of them had been working late into the night trying to get the prototype working. They had an upcoming presentation with NFA and they wanted to show the prototype to impress them.

"How is the Cadence team coming along?" asked John.

"Could be better," replied Tricia in a slightly dejected tone. "We are encountering many challenges."

"I see," continued John. "Tricia, instead of the usual imparting of knowledge, how about we try something different. Let's have a coaching conversation on your situation."

"Ok," said Tricia looking puzzled.

"Great! Let's begin," said John as both of them settled down. "Tricia, what would you like to discuss?"

"Well, we have a number of challenges. We have to figure out a good value proposition for the upcoming NFA presentation. We also need to solve the technical issue that we are facing with the prototype. On top of that, we have some people issues with the team," replied Tricia.

"That is quite a handful of issues," John said. "Given the limited time, in the next forty-five minutes, which issue would you like to focus on?"

Tricia thought for a while. "Perhaps we can discuss on the people issue. It is more challenging compared to the rest."

"Ok. Tell me more about the people issue," asked John.

"Well, there are these two software developers. They are not getting along with each other. They seem to be going at each other's throats all the time, to the extent that it is affecting the entire project. I am at a loss as to how to handle this. I was wondering if I should get Gary involved," said Tricia.

"I see," said John. "At the end of this session, what would you like to take away?"

After a short pause, Tricia replied, "Come up with one or two ideas to resolve this conflict."

"Good! So, your goal is to derive one or two ways to resolve the conflict," said John. "What do you think is causing this conflict?"

"Well, there is this senior software developer, Liu Jian, who is very experienced in integrating the various technology together. The other developer is Suresh, who is the expert in the blockchain technology. Suresh is always behind in his delivery schedule. This is frustrating Liu Jian as he needs Suresh's portion to test out the prototype at different stages. Liu Jian has repeatedly complained to me about Suresh and has suggested that we replace Suresh with another person from Gary's team.

"I have spoken to Suresh but things are not improving. He is a hardworking guy, very talented. In fact, he personally told me he was very excited to be a part of the Cadence team. I do not want to demotivate him by taking him out of the team. But if I don't, it will affect the whole project schedule," said Tricia.

"What are the possible reasons Suresh is missing the deadline?" asked John curiously.

"Maybe it could be a cultural thing," said Tricia. "Suresh joined the company from India about six months ago. Perhaps he does not understand the importance of meeting deadline. I know Suresh is a very detailed person. He will make sure all the software codes are tested properly before passing over to Liu Jian. My guess is that he is a perfectionist.

"The other reason could be communication problem. After all, Liu Jian is from China and his command of English is not as strong. So, Suresh could be misinterpreting Liu Jian's request."

"Any other reasons that you can think of?" asked John.

Tricia pondered over the question. "The other possibility is that Liu Jian is not a very organized person. He lacks structure in the project schedule and he can make changes whenever he feels like it. Because of that, Suresh could be fed up with him. Coupled with their lack of communication, it has worsened the situation."

"That's quite a good insight, Tricia. Given your awareness now, how would you handle the situation differently?" asked John.

"I think I'll get Liu Jian to come up with a more structured project schedule. Then I will call for a team meeting with the relevant parties. In that meeting, we will get everyone to commit to the delivery schedule. Any changes to the schedule has to be agreed by everyone. Since my command of English and Mandarin is reasonably good, I can minimize the miscommunication," said Tricia.

"Any other options?" John asked.

"I guess I would have to speak to both Liu Jian and Suresh. Get them to understand how best to work with each other. Liu Jian has to be aware that Suresh doesn't like ad hoc changes. Likewise, Suresh needs to understand the importance of keeping to the timeline and the impact to the entire project. Moreover, I have to make him realise that we don't need to have a perfect module at this prototype stage. He will have time to improve it when we have the buy-in from NFA," replied Tricia.

"So, Tricia, you came up with two ways to handle the situation. Firstly, to have a more structured project schedule and a follow-on meeting to communicate to everyone. And secondly, to speak to both of them," continued John. "How would you like to proceed?"

"I can speak to both of them this afternoon," said Tricia with a more confident tone. "I'll get Liu Jian to come out with a proper project schedule by this week. We can then schedule a team meeting next week. I guess I will have to speak to each of them individually to get their buy-in."

"That sounds great!" exclaimed John. "Was this session helpful for you?"

"Definitely, John," said Tricia. "I have more clarity of the situation now. This has been bothering me for a few weeks and has caused me to delay working on the value proposition for the project.

"I guess I can even use this coaching approach with the team members whenever they face challenges."

"Absolutely!" said John. "Just remember to use the T-GROW process in your conversation."

"T-GROW!" asked Tricia inquisitively.

"Yes, T-GROW is a popular coaching process used by many leader coaches.

"T stands for *Topic*. The topic is the situation or problem that the coachee brings up in the discussion. As a leader coach, you could start off the conversation by asking the coachee what he or she wants to discuss.

"G stands for *Goal*. You will need to ask your coachee what he or she wants to achieve by the end of the discussion. Otherwise, both of you could be talking the whole day without getting anywhere.

"R stands for *Reality*. It is about what the current situation is and how far he or she is from the goal. You can also explore their current thinking, assumptions, beliefs and emotions.

"O refers to *Options*. This is where you get the coachee to explore the different options or possibilities to overcome the challenge.

"Finally, W is for the *Way forward*. Once you have explored the various options, that's when the coachee decides on which approach to take. Essentially, these are the actions to be taken by the coachee.

"Noticed that in our conversation, you came up with the options. Likewise, you decided on the actions to move forward."

"That's right, John," said Tricia. "I am more motivated to carry out the actions because I came out with them, rather than you telling me what to do. Awesome!"

"Keep me updated on the progress. And if you have any problems, you know where to find me!" John said laughingly.

The **T-GROW** process provides a structured coaching conversation. Start off by asking the coachee to share more about the **Topic** of discussion before identifying the **Goal** or outcome. Explore the **Reality** of the situation, and the **Options** available. Take actions by getting the coachee to commit on the **Way forward**.

23.

BUILDING ON DIFFERENCES

Everyone was standing in front of the meeting room eyes glued to the projection screen. They were studying the chart closely where they were in relation to the rest of the team. John was showing the management the team wheel. He had the agreement from Victor to conduct a behavioral analysis on the management team.

"Now that each of you has seen your own behavioral analysis report of your natural and adaptive style, the chart over here shows the team wheel. This team wheel shows where you are in relation to the rest of the team when you are using your adaptive style," John said.

"The chart shows some interesting facts," John continued. "Notice that all of you are spread across the whole chart. In short, this team has personalities well represented across all the four quadrants. For example, Gary is in the 'D' Dominance quadrant, AK in 'I' Influence, Din in 'S' Steadiness and Serene in 'C' Conscientiousness.

Some of you have a combination of behavioral styles, so you will see yourself in between.

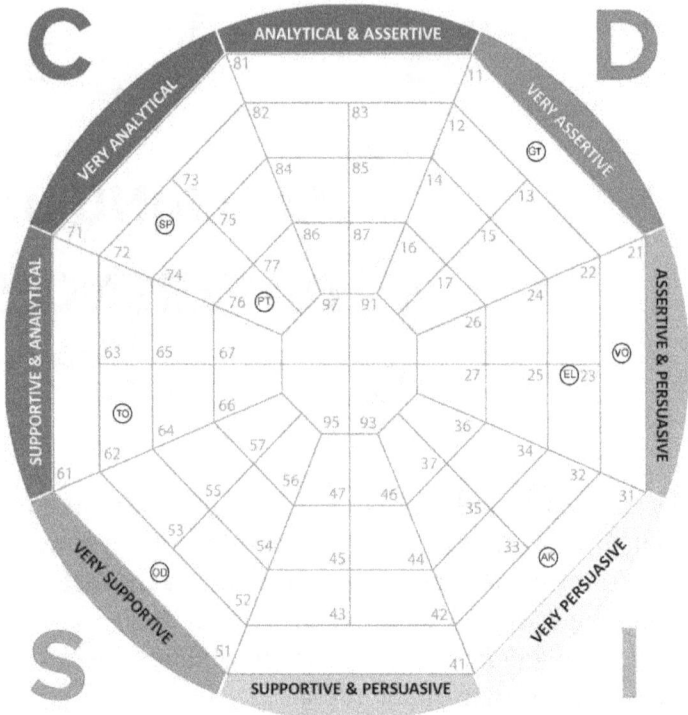

DISC Behavioral Analysis Team Wheel of IRS Management Team

"What is interesting is that most of you are adapting to the styles that most suit your job role. Din, let's take your case. You are in the 'S' quadrant, which demonstrates that you are a supportive person. And that's really what you do for the company in the operations department. You support the organization just like a defender in the football team!" John said as both Din and him laughed.

"For AK, you are an 'I' personality, which suits well with your role in marketing as you need to be creative and outgoing to influence the internal team and the customers on the company's product offerings. Likewise Serene, your attention to details as a 'C' person is useful for your finance role."

"This is quite interesting. But what does it mean if we are on opposite ends of the chart?" asked Victor.

John had expected that question to come out when he first saw the chart as he noticed that Victor and Tricia were on opposite sides. Perhaps that is the reason why they have had a number of arguments, John thought.

"That is a good question, Victor," continued John. "The reason why I wanted to conduct this exercise is to get everyone to realize that we are all different. Each of us has our own strengths. We leverage on our strengths to achieve our goals. For many of us, when we understand our strengths and personality, we tend to gravitate to the job roles that best suit us. Let's take the case of Serene. She is a 'C' person, which means that she is one who likes data and facts, accuracy, standards and rules to name a few. These traits are key for a finance person.

"We need people with different personalities and strengths to make a great organization. If all of you are skewed to a particular quadrant, it may mean that the organization is lacking in some capabilities.

"So, coming back to Victor's question, the key here is how do we build on the differences? That is the most important part of this entire exercise. If I may use Serene as an example again. All of you know that she is one who likes details and accuracy. When Eric or AK, who may not be very detailed, sends in orders or information in bits and pieces, or even worst wrong information, guess how she would feel? She would probably scream at them!

"Now I understand why you are always screaming at my team!" said Eric jokingly as Serene smiled sheepishly.

"Likewise, a 'D' person who is very task oriented would expect jobs to be completed quickly. The 'D' person may view the 'S' person, who tends to be more structured, steady and people oriented, to be slow and uncommitted. In other words, if Eric's sales team throws a last-minute order to the operations team and expects it to be delivered the next moment, Din is not going to like it!

"So, it is important to understand the preferences of the person and the do's and don'ts. In that way, you will learn to work with each other and get the best out of the other person," added John.

"I'm curious, John, in our personal report there is a natural and an adaptive style. If it shows that my natural and adaptive style is on opposite sides, what does that mean?" asked Paul.

"It means you are Dr. Jekyll and Mr. Hyde, Paul," Din said jokingly.

"Yes, it does happen. When you are in your work

environment, your job may require you to adapt to a style that is different from your natural style. For example, when you are at home at your most natural self, you may enjoy a more carefree and outgoing style. But when you come to work and the job requires you to be more detailed and structured, you would likely adapt to that style. For some people, they may find tension or difficulty adjusting between the two styles. For others, they are perfectly fine with it.

"Bear in mind that our styles may change over time depending on the environment that we are in," said John.

At the end of the meeting, everyone left the room in high energy, disturbing each other as to how they should work with each other moving forward. John took out his notebook and wrote down "6. Building on Differences (Din)" as he recalled how this exercise started because of his discussion with Din.

In a Nutshell

*A high-performance team requires people with **different personalities and strengths**. The key is learning how to **work with these differences** and leverage on each other's strength.*

24

QUIET TIME

It was a late Friday afternoon at the end of May. Paul had just shared with John on his plan for the team. He had wanted to get John's opinion prior to bringing up to Victor for approval. John was happy to see that Paul had found the time to work on the plan. In fact, Paul shared with John that he had taken his advice on asking powerful questions. Now, it seems that his team is more independent.

John could see that his efforts were paying off. Just early in the week, Eric had told him that his relationship with his two younger sales representatives has improved tremendously. This was after he shifted his mindset and started to empower them to take their own actions. He also mentioned that the materials put together by Tricia was very useful for his team. They are now more confident to engage with the clients.

As John took a walk around the office, he noticed the posters of "The A-Team" from the original movie of the same name being pinned around the operations department. He thought to himself, "Wow, Din is really serious about his Class A & B student story!"

As he passed by the demonstration room, he saw Tricia with three of the software developers in deep discussion. They looked very exhausted as if they have not slept for a number of days. John decided to interrupt.

"Hi guys! How is the prototype app coming along?" asked John.

Tricia and the three developers looked up at John in a surprised but weary look. "It is not going too well," said Tricia. "Our final presentation to NFA is on Tuesday. And we are unable to solve the problem. It is important that we show this working app to NFA. Hopefully they will be convinced to include our key differentiating features in the tender specs."

"And we haven't had much sleep the whole of this week," Suresh chipped in.

"Yes, Suresh needs lots of sleep. Otherwise he can't think!" said Liu Jian teasingly.

It seems that the relationship between Suresh and Liu Jian has improved, John thought to himself as they were both laughing together. Tricia must have done a good job coaching both of them.

"Perhaps, Liu Jian brought up a good suggestion," John continued. "Sometimes when we are too tired, our minds become clouded. When that happens, no matter how hard we bang our head against the wall, we are not able to find the right solution. When we rest our minds, you will be surprised the answers might just pop up! That is what usually happens to me.

"Just the other day, I came across an article. It was an interview with an English teacher. This teacher was a soldier with the British army during World War II. They were in the jungles of Burma and one day, one of the scouts came running back to them. The scout told them that they were surrounded by large troops of Japanese soldiers. There was no way out for them. They were a small troop but all the soldiers were determined not to be captured, but to fight till they die. At least they would have killed some of the enemies along the way.

"The soldiers turned to the captain for the battle plan. To their shock, the captain told them to stay put, sit down and make themselves a cup of tea. Well, in those days, they have to follow orders and that's what they did. Shortly after, the scout came back and told the captain that the enemy has moved, and there was a way out. Immediately, the captain ordered the men to pack up and escape quietly. To this day, that teacher has told his family and friends that he owed his life to the wisdom of his captain."

"Awesome," said Tricia.

"Yes, sometimes you need that quiet time. Let it rest. You don't always have to fight all the time!" said John.

"Yes, guys. I agree with John. Let's call it a day and come back on Monday. There is no point continuing given that all of us are so tired," said Tricia as they started to pack up.

John bade farewell to them as he decided to call it a day as well.

In a Nutshell

*Some of the most **creative** and **innovative ideas** come when we allow our minds to rest or during **silent moments**.*

25.

LIFELONG LEARNING

It was just after lunch on Tuesday afternoon and John had just parked his car. He had spent the morning at an orientation programme conducted by one of the government agencies. As he was walking towards the office building, he met Tricia, Jessica and a few of the other guys. They had just returned from their presentation at NFA.

"How did the presentation go?" asked John.

"It went very well. Thanks to you, John!" said Tricia.

"Thanks to me?" asked John in a puzzled tone as they entered the lift.

"Yes, John. You remember the conversation we had last Friday afternoon about spending quiet time," continued Tricia. "I did just that on Friday evening and Saturday, not thinking about the project. On Sunday morning, as I was having breakfast, an idea came out of nowhere. I called the guys about the possibility of the workaround, and we were back in the office that afternoon. By Sunday night, we had the prototype app working!"

"Yeah. The whole Saturday of sleeping really energized me," said Suresh cheerfully.

"Yup, Suresh was in full form on Sunday!" Liu Jian teasing Suresh as usual.

"Wow. I am glad that helped!" John answered.

"NFA was really impressed with what we demonstrated. Jessica and I are going to put together the list of features and benefits. Hopefully, they will include that in the tender specs," said Tricia.

"I am so happy for you guys. Keep it up!" said John encouragingly as they walked into the office. John headed to his usual meeting room and Serene was already there. She was the last of the management team that John had yet to meet up for a one-on-one session. She had been busy closing up the accounts for the last financial year and getting all the necessary sign-offs from the company directors.

"Hi, Serene. Finally, we get the chance to sit down together," John said. "I heard that you are the longest serving employee!"

Serene laughed as she told John that she has been with the company for twenty two years. She joined right after college as she could not get into university. She had started off as the personal assistant to Victor handling all his administrative and accounting work. Over the years, she studied part time for her accounting degree. She finally received her accounting degree at the age of 30 and went on to get her MBA at the age of 38, just two years ago.

"You are truly an example of what the government has always encouraged: lifelong learning!" John said enthusiastically.

Lifelong learning

"In fact, I have been recently roped in by the government to help our local SMEs. I just completed the last of the orientation programme this morning. This government initiative is called SkillsFuture Mentor programme. Our role as mentors are to help SMEs improve their learning and development capabilities for their employees. The ultimate goal is to help them build a robust system and process to enable their employees to upskill themselves to meet the challenges they face. Just like what you have been doing over the years. You have the right mindset of lifelong learning. The only difference is that you are personally motivated to learn on your own. Not every employee is like you. I am quite sure the company doesn't have a system in place to enable your learning, right?"

"That's true. I guess part of my role as a HR manager is to look into that as well. But where do I start?" asked Serene.

"Well, there is a diagnostics tool which we call HR Maturity Diagnostics (HRMD) that you can use to understand the current HR maturity level of the company and determine the gaps," continued John. "Besides training and development, it helps to analyze areas such as performance management, compensation and benefits, talent management, recruitment, organization culture and many more."

John continued, "Victor has shared with us his vision and goals. One of his goals is people development. And he is right. This company is built on people. Without recruiting the right talent and continuously developing its employees, this company can never progress far.

"When we talk about learning and development, it is not just about providing ad-hoc training to the employees. It has to be a systematic approach. All the leaders have heard the vision from Victor, and they know where we need to be. They have to find out the skills that are required to get there, and to analyze the current gaps in their team. Once they have performed their training needs analysis, they will be able to map out the development plan for each of their team members. And it need not be just pure classroom training. There are many other learning approaches that one can take."

John noticed that Serene had been busy taking down notes as he spoke. He could sense that she was still clueless as to what she should work on first.

In a Nutshell

*One of the most **important assets** for an organization is **people**. Investing in this asset is about **developing the people** to be future-ready.*

26.

SYSTEMS AND PROCESSES

"So Serene, coming back to your question on where you should start," continued John. "We know that learning and development is one of our key goals. Perhaps we can focus on that first. It is important that we put in place the necessary systems and processes to enable the leaders and the employees.

"We don't really need to have an expensive system to begin with. Previously when I was working in the MNCs, we used to have those popular and expensive performance management systems. However, I do understand for SME companies like IRS with no critical mass, it may not be practical to acquire such a system immediately. You could start off with some simple electronic documentation template for all the departments to use. For example, you could design a learning and development plan (LDP) template for the company. All the leaders can use this LDP template to discuss the learning actions for the year with their team. In this way, the leaders will know what needs to be done and it will provide consistency across the company.

"Besides coming out with the templates, it is also important to outline the process clearly so that everyone knows what to do. I am sure you have a standard operation procedure (SOP) for the employees to submit their expense claim. Likewise, you would need to define the SOP for the learning and development process. The good thing about the process is that you can specify timelines for submissions. For example, you can ask the leaders to provide a consolidated view of the training requirements for their department by a certain date. This will allow you to prioritize and plan the entire organization training calendar for the year."

"So, we can avoid ad-hoc trainings and reduce unnecessary training cost," said Serene.

"That is correct!" continued John. "Remember, classroom training may not be the only means of learning. Employees can learn through online, self-learning or join their industry or professional association. They can also learn via on-the-job training by shadowing a more experienced co-worker. In some companies, they form community of practice where like-minded individuals come together on a regular basis to share their views, challenges and learn from each other."

"That is quite a whole lot of stuff that needs to be done just for learning and development! And I have only three staff. One who handles the accounts, the other who does payroll, expense claims and some HR administration, and of course our senior receptionist!" exclaimed Serene.

"Don't worry, Serene. Learning and development is not the sole responsibility of HR department. Your role is to develop the systems and processes for the organization. The leaders have to take responsibility for developing their team members, by leveraging on the systems and processes. Of course, they have to be trained in managing the systems and processes, which I call 'hard' skill. There is also the 'soft' skill aspect of leadership that they would also need to be trained in. This involves the coaching of their team members.

"If we take a holistic approach, the ultimate goal is to drive the performance of the employees to meet the company's objectives. Training is just one aspect of driving performance. The company would also have to look at other non-training factors like compensation and rewards, career progression and employee engagement programme."

"I would seriously have to speak to Victor about increasing my department headcount!" said Serene laughingly. "You are right. We need to look into all the different aspect of how we engage our employees. It is getting very challenging for us to hire good talent, especially the younger employees. We need to build a good branding for the company, one that develops people so that we can attract and retain the best talent."

Before they ended the meeting, John agreed to help Serene to develop the LDP template and process. They also agreed to jointly conduct the training for the leaders that cover both the 'hard' skill of managing the systems and processes, as well as the leadership coaching 'soft' skill.

When John finished writing down the list of things to do, he turned to his favorite page and drew a big circle around his six characteristics that he had written so far. On the big circle, he wrote "Systems and Processes (Serene Pereira)."

In a Nutshell

As a **leader**, you will need the "hard skill" of **managing systems and processes**, as well as the "soft skill" of **leading people**.

27.

ASIAN MANAGEMENT STYLE

It was already in the middle of July as John and Tricia sat down for a discussion.

"Look at how the time flies. I can't believe I have been here for five months already!" John said. "Anyway, I've heard that NFA has called for the tender?"

"Yes, that is correct," replied Tricia. "And they did include some of the features that we had proposed, not everything though. We definitely have a shot at this. In fact, some of the local banks and financial institutions have called us. They want to partner with us in the tender."

"That is great news!" said John excitedly. "They probably got the word on the street as to which horse to bet on!"

Tricia laughed as she continued, "And just yesterday, Jessica told me that one of the major mobile platform suppliers called her asking if they can bid with us. But we have a lot of work ahead of us in the next few months.

I would also need to increase the headcount for the Cadence team. Although that will be a challenge for Gary."

"I see. Tell me more about the situation," asked John.

"Well, I sounded out to him that I needed an additional person from his team to help out during this tender period. I could sense that he was not happy and has yet to get back to me," said Tricia.

"Why do you think he is not happy?" asked John.

"My guess is that he might have a lack of resource as well. Liu Jian and Suresh had proposed a particular developer to join the team. They said that guy is quite good and does not seem to be fully occupied most of the time. But of course, they might not have the full picture," said Tricia.

"What other reasons could there be?" John asked curiously.

Tricia paused for a while and said, "Could it be because he feels like losing control of his team?"

"That is a possibility," replied John.

"But, he should not worry about that. He will get his whole team back once the tender is completed!" Tricia said matter-of-factly.

John then shared with Tricia his experience working with the different types of managers in Asia. There are those who feel the need to be respected and in control of everything. These managers are likely to have come from a background of strict and disciplined parenting. Their parents will always be there to provide for and protect them. In turn, they are expected to respect their parents and not question anything they are told to do. There are still a number of Asian managers who have been conditioned in such an environment and apply the same principles in managing their teams.

On the other hand, because of past Asian policies and

economic circumstances, there are families with very few or just one or two kids. The parents treat their only child like precious diamond, not daring to scold them when they have done something wrong. Managers who come from this type of background may find it difficult to give tough feedback to their team members. They would rather leave the poor performers as they are, hoping that they will somehow get better.

Tricia nodded as she reflected on the styles of the management team. She could deduce which managers fall under the two styles that John had just mentioned.

"Of course, not every manager falls into those two categories. Besides upbringing and conditioning, organizations have a key part to play as well," continued John. "Many organizations promote their managers without giving them the necessary training. Organizations are very good at coming up with systems and processes. They trained the managers on how to use the tools to measure productivity, output and monitor the results. They put in place processes, policies and guidelines for the managers to enforce their employees to comply accordingly. The one and most important skill of learning how to deal with people seems to be ignored.

"Personally, I have seen companies promote a good individual contributor to a managerial role just because they needed to fill a vacant position. No formal training is provided. A few months later, the senior management may hear complaints about the new manager. They will quickly deduce that this manager is not of managerial quality and reassign him or her to other special projects. We all know what usually happens with such managers. They will become demotivated and leave the company. Basically, the company has promoted a competent individual to a position of incompetence. At the end of the day, the company have lost a valuable employee.

"The good news is that some organisations are realizing the importance of leadership soft skills training. Leadership coaching is an approach that many Asian leaders are beginning to adopt. Whether they have a disciplined or doted-upon conditioning, applying the coaching skills has helped the managers build a bridge with their employees."

John noticed that Tricia was deep in thoughts. After a while, she said, "It will probably take some time for the managers to pick up the coaching skills and to change their mindset. Given the urgency of this tender, I guess I would have to find alternative ways of getting my resources."

John smiled as he looked at Tricia, "Or, you could change your perspective of the situation!"

"Change my perspective?" queried Tricia.

"Yes, how we view our situation vary from person to person. If we view it in a negative way, that everything is going against us, we are disempowering ourselves. However, if we choose to take a positive view of the same situation, then we have the ability to empower ourselves," John continued.

"Take for instance Gary's case. Now that you understand why he could be behaving that way, and that it is not because he wants to make it difficult for you, what would you do differently if you were to look from the positive lens?"

Change our perspective of the situation to be more empowering

"Tricia pondered over the question and said "I guess if he is afraid of losing control of his team, I could reassure him upfront that would not be the case. I might even let him know that once we win the tender, we would be adding more headcount to his team.

"In fact, you have given me an idea. We have a request from the local university to take in two intern students starting next month. We could attach them to Gary's department to help alleviate any lack of resource concern he might have. If we train these interns well, we might even have the opportunity to hire them when they graduate the following year."

"You are on a roll, Tricia!" John said excitedly.

"Thanks, John. You are right again as always," continued Tricia. "I guess if we change our perspective to be more empowering, we will become more creative and resourceful in addressing the challenge. Between the situation and me, nothing has changed. It is just a question of how I want to view and approach the situation!"

In a Nutshell

*We may not always be able to change the situation or other people's behavior. However, we can **change our perspective** of the situation to be more **empowering** for us.*

28.

WHO BEARS RESPONSIBILITY

It was a long weekend on a Sunday afternoon in September. John was at home working on the presentation materials for the IRS management team.

Over the course of the last eight months, John had built up the list of characteristics of a high-performance team. As he reviewed through the materials, a key question keeps popping up in his mind.

"Who bears the responsibility of ensuring the success of the company?" John asked himself.

"Is it the CEO or MD who should bear the responsibility? Or should all the managers bear the responsibility? Perhaps the employees or the Bear himself!" John thought to himself laughingly as he imagined pointing the finger at the bear.

He decided to go through each of the characteristics of a high-performance team (HPT).

Aligned Vision and Goals

Obviously, the CEO has to set the vision and goals for the company, with inputs from the board of directors or key management staff. Once the vision and goals are established, the managers need to align their department goals and plans accordingly. The vision and goals would also need to be communicated to the employees to ensure that everyone is aware of the destination.

Empowerment

HPT leaders need to have the mindset to:

- Be a Facilitator, not an Advisor
- Believe that employees are creative and resourceful
- Focus on their strengths, rather than their weaknesses

With the right mindset, leaders can empower their team members by creating awareness and facilitating self-discovery. When the employees feel empowered, they will become responsible and accountable for their actions.

Trust

In order for the leaders to coach their team members, trust has to be built between both parties. This involves competency trust which can be demonstrated through one's abilities or credentials. The other which takes time to build is character trust, which is based on sincerity, authenticity and honesty.

Trust between team members is also important in a high-performance team. Each one depends on the other for support and encouragement. Once there is a lack of trust, the team will not be able to perform at its peak.

Communication

Effective communication is critical between the leader and the team members. Communication is a two-way process that involves active listening and powerful questioning.

Active listening involves being open and curious to what the other party is saying. One would have to listen to both the content and the context of the topic. Besides listening with all your senses, one can also paraphrase and ask clarifying questions to listen actively.

Powerful questioning involves asking more open-ended questions to help the coachee think, reflect and decide. The leader can structure the questions with the intent of challenging the coachee's assumptions or beliefs, to evoke confidence or to help the coachee expand his or her perspectives.

Communication between team members is also as important. When communication breaks down between the members, problems will surface and results will be affected.

Growth Mindset

Every employee in the organization needs to have a growth mindset. They must believe that capabilities can be developed. Organisation can only grow when employees have a lifelong learning mindset.

Employees who have a fixed mindset will rarely seek out opportunities to learn or challenge themselves. They have a fear of failure as that will reflect upon their abilities which they view as fixed. As a result, organizations with fixed mindset employees will struggle to improve.

Building on Differences

Everyone is unique with his or her own strengths and abilities. The famous Greek philosopher Aristotle says, "The Whole is Greater than the Sum of its Parts." When the organization is able to build on the strengths and abilities of every individual, it will be able to achieve much more.

Members of HPT are aware of their own styles. They can identify and recognize the styles of others and adapt to the different styles. They develop ways to communicate effectively and leverage on each other's strengths. Through this synergy, high-performance teams are able to deliver much better results.

Systems and Processes

The systems and processes of an organization provide a framework for all employees to leverage on. For any given task, it is important to have a process which specifies what the input is, the sequence of events and the eventual output. When we look at the process, we are addressing the effectiveness of that task.

For example, when employees apply for vacation, there is usually a process that they have to follow. Typically, employees would have to submit the leave application to their manager for approval. Upon approval, their leave application will be forwarded to the HR department for records update.

Systems, on the other hand, are a set of tools and technologies that help to improve the efficiency and productivity of any given task. So, in the case of the leave application example, organisations could use automated systems where everything can be submitted and approved through a computer system. This helps to eliminate the paperwork trail, provide up-to-date leave balance information and most importantly speed up the whole process.

The pitfall for many organisations is the over reliance on systems and processes. Managers of such organisations would be spending all their working hours managing their teams through these systems, monitoring the KPIs. They forget that at the end of the day, they are dealing with people.

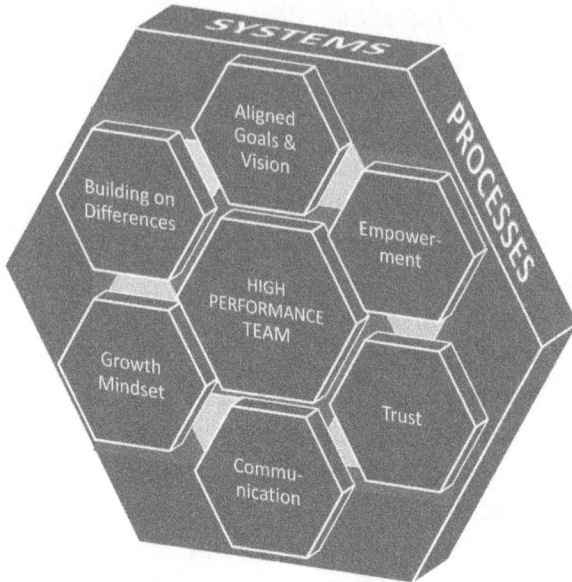

Characteristics of High-Performance Team (HPT)

As John looked at the model that he had designed, he knew that everyone has a part to play in building a high-performance team. Of course, it would have to start from the management team. He wrote down the following sentence so that he can remind the management team.

MANAGE systems and processes. LEAD people

29.

DECISION

John was just wrapping up his meeting with Serene when Tricia burst into the room. There she was in her usual white T-shirt and black jeans, grinning from ear to ear.

"We have won!" she shouted. "NFA has just officially sent us their decision on the tender."

"Congratulations!" echoed Serene and John.

"Thanks!" replied Tricia. "Actually, Jessica and I did get some unofficial word two days ago. But we did not dare to tell anybody until we get the official letter from NFA. I can't wait to tell the team. I wanted to share the good news with you first. You have been a great help to me and my team, John. Thanks so much!"

"You are welcome, Tricia. You should have a big celebration!" said John.

"Yes, I was thinking of inviting the team out for dinner and drinks tonight together with the management team. Would both of you be able to join us?"

"Sure!" said Serene excitedly. "It is TGIF after all!"

"I wish I could, but I have another dinner appointment.

Please go ahead and enjoy yourself. You guys deserve it! Please send my wishes to the team," said John.

"I will. Thanks again," replied Tricia.

Later in the evening, John was sharing the great news with May. It was their twentieth anniversary and they were having dinner at a nice Japanese restaurant.

"Tricia must be so happy!" said May.

"Yes, she is overjoyed," John continued. "Although she may not realise it, she needed that win to earn the trust and confidence with the team. Now, the management team and the employees will have more confidence in her if she eventually takes over from Victor."

"Congratulations to you as well, dear!" said May smiling. "You have really helped the company grow. And I can see that you have enjoyed your journey with them as well."

"Yes, it has been a fulfilling year working with them. To be able to leverage on my corporate experience and help SMEs like them was very satisfying," continued John. "I wish you could experience that as well."

There was a moment of silence. May spoke, "Actually, I have been thinking for a while now. The amount of travelling that I have been doing is taking a toll on me. On top of that, the numbers keep increasing. I don't know how long I can continue working in the corporate?"

John thought for a while and said, "Why don't we start our own management consulting business? Your past twenty-five years of corporate experience managing the Asia Pacific business is an asset. You have been coaching leaders from different cultural backgrounds. These credentials will definitely help to build our company profile.

"You could also take on the role of a SkillsFuture Mentor just like what I did and help the local SMEs. I have already created some training materials that we can use to provide training and coaching to the organisations out there. Like I shared with you the other day, there are already two large organisations that are interested to engage me for next year to train and coach their leaders. You could share the job with me so that it won't be too strenuous on me. Besides, I don't think we should be working the way we did in the corporate. We should be spending more time together."

"How does that sound?" asked John excitedly.

"Wow, it is kind of a big change stepping out of the corporate and starting on your own. It does sound exciting although scary!" said May.

"Well, we were fortunate enough to be around when the companies and the industry were growing rapidly. We have had our share of good times, some challenging years but generally many good years. Now is perhaps a good time for us to give back to society. To help the local SMEs as well as the younger generation of leaders in the corporate. If you look from that angle, this is a good thing," said John.

"I guess if you look at it that way, it makes sense," replied May.

"So, what is your decision?" asked John curiously.

"Let me have a conference call with my boss next week. Not too sure if he will let me go, but I will try and convince him," said May.

"Great! Let's have a toast. Happy Anniversary!" said John as they both clinked their cup of Japanese tea!

In a Nutshell

Life is a journey. The best *gift* in life is to *give* back what you have learned and gained along the way.

30.

PARTY TIME

As John walked into IRS office on a cool and drizzly day, he noticed the buzz of activities. People were chatting around their cubicles while others were busy preparing for the Christmas party. John greeted many of the familiar faces as he headed to Victor's office.

John knocked on the door. Victor and Tricia turned around and greeted John.

"Merry Christmas! Hope I am not interrupting?" said John.

"No, John. We have already ended our meeting. I knew you were coming, so I decided to hang around for a while just to greet you," Tricia said joyfully as she took her leave.

"John, so good to see you again," continued Victor. "I have been travelling so much over the last few months that I haven't had the chance to catch up with you."

"So, how are the other countries coming along?" John asked.

"Well, I have met up with a lot of my networks in those countries as well as some potential customers. I have decided to open two offices next year, one in Vietnam, the other in Cambodia. For Myanmar, we will go into a joint-venture with a local distributor," said Victor.

"That sounds very exciting. I am so happy things are moving in the right direction. With that big NFA win, the growth potential for the company looks promising," said John.

"Many thanks to you, John. You have been a great help to the entire team, especially Tricia. Things would not be where it is today without your support," Victor said humbly.

"You are welcome, Victor. I believe it is a team effort. All I did was to coach them to make their own decisions and to take responsibility," continued John. "I am so happy Tricia has grown in maturity over the last year. She is a fast learner and I can see the team's growing confidence in her."

"Yes, John. You have also helped me change my view of her. Our relationship has definitely improved since then. In fact, we just had a meeting this morning just before you came in. AK will be leaving us at the end of the month. I guess he still wants to be an entrepreneur. He is joining a couple of his old buddies in a startup venture. Because of that, I have decided to make Tricia as our Chief Strategy Officer (CSO) taking care of the company's strategy, marketing and business development as well as to start a new technology research and development group.

"What we did with the Cadence project team is a wonderful idea. So we have decided to form a special project team to focus on new technology. The blockchain technology we developed for the NFA project can be further enhanced for use in many other industries like the supply chain, property and even the Internet of Things (IoT).

"Given Tricia's knowledge of technology, I guess she is

the right person for the job. I am from the dinosaur age," Victor laughed.

"I totally agree with you. This will be a good move for her and hopefully in a year or two, she will be ready to be the CEO!" said John excitedly. "But how do you think Gary will take this?"

"Well, Gary will continue to lead the software development group and continue to enhance our existing product lines. I can see that he is improving in his leadership skills, thanks to you. I believe he has his strengths and will be more suited to work on improving on what we have. Tricia is more open and creative. So, leading the new technology and our business strategy plays more to her strengths," said Victor confidently.

"That is great!" continued John. "Victor, I wanted to talk to you about our part-time contract. We are coming towards the end of our contract and I believe your team is equipped and ready. May and I have decided to start our own management consulting business focusing on leadership training and coaching. In fact, she will be leaving her corporate job at the end of next month.

"I have also been recently assigned an SME company as part of my SkillsFuture Mentor role. That project will be starting in January so I wanted to see if you are agreeable for my part-time contract to end by this month."

"First of all. Congratulations! I am so happy for you and May. I truly believe both of you will make a great team," Victor continued.

"For the contract sure, we can end this month. I will inform Serene. However, can I engage you to continue to coach Tricia? It can be a once-a-month session over the next six to nine months period. I believe with her new role, she would definitely face challenges and would probably need some support. You are the best person I can think of. And I would think she will be delighted to have you as her personal coach! Just don't charge me too high, though," said Victor laughingly.

"I will be delighted to coach Tricia! And yes, I will go easy with my coaching fee, just for you," John smiled.

"It is party time!" said Victor as both of them headed to the meeting room where they were having the Christmas lunch party.

As he scanned around the room, he could see the many happy and familiar faces. Many of them came over to greet him.

At the end of the party, as John walked towards his car, he thought to himself.

"We were once strangers, trying to work with each other. Now less than a year later, we have become good friends. It has also been a privilege to see them develop into a high-performance team."

He felt a tinge of sadness knowing he would not be around that often moving forward. However, as he thought about what is coming ahead, he felt a great sense of excitement.

"What will the next part of the journey bring forth?"

In a Nutshell

*Whether you are leading a small team or a large organization, it is important to **care** for your team members. When you care, building and **leading a High-Performance Team** will be one of the **greatest joys** in your life journey.*

ABOUT THE AUTHORS

Laurence TAN

Well recognized as a "Difference Maker", Laurence currently dedicates his time to help professionals and businesses excel in their goals through his Coaching and Training services. He has more than 25 years of industry experience. These include roles in General Management and Sales/ Technical Management with US Multi-National Companies (MNCs) in the high tech industry (IT/ Engineering), as well as an Entrepreneur in the Retail/ Distribution and Management Consulting/ Coaching industries. He graduated with a Bachelors Degree in Electrical Engineering from the National University of Singapore and was an "Asia International Executive Program" graduate from INSEAD Business School. Laurence is a Certified SkillsFuture Mentor with Enterprise Singapore and an International Coach Federation, ICF Certified Coach.

In his role as SkillsFuture Mentor, Laurence helps local SMEs develop future ready employees to meet their business goals. He works with the Owners/HR/Leaders to perform learning needs analysis, review and develop systems and processes. Leveraging on his leadership coaching skills, he has coached and mentored SME leaders in various industries including Finance (Fintech), Information Technology, Engineering, Chemical Distribution, FMCG and Manufacturing sectors.

During his time working in Corporate and SMEs, Laurence was very much involved in the Talent Development and Performance Management of his team. His ability to understand Business & Performance Needs, and building the Team's Competency to drive business goals, has been the key to his success. This has led him to win multiple top Asia Pacific Business and Life Achievement Awards.

C. Eng Neo

Eng Neo currently dedicates her time to coaching and training Senior Executives, Leaders and Business Owners to unleash their maximum potential, effect change and improve organizational performance.

She is a seasoned Business Leader & practical Coach with more than twenty-five years of experience working with clients in multiple Industries and Segments (Large Enterprises, SMEs and Public sector). Her more than twenty years of Leadership experience spans across General Management, Business and Sales Management in Corporate Multi-national Companies (MNCs) such as IBM as well as Small and Medium Enterprises (SMEs). With her results-focused approach, coaching & collaborative style, she has guided many individuals and teams to great successes. For her contributions, she has been recognized with numerous Achievement awards such as Asia Pacific General

Manager's award, Asia Pacific Passion for Growth, Top Leader award and more.

She supports the nationwide SkillsFuture initiative as a SkillsFuture Mentor to SMEs. In this capacity, Eng Neo works with SMEs to develop future ready leaders and employees. With her experience and understanding of their business needs, she helps them to develop the relevant people competencies to achieve their goals.

Eng Neo is an ICF Certified Coach (International Coach Federation) and a Certified Master Performance Coach. She graduated with a Bachelor of Engineering (Hons) degree from the National University of Singapore and has completed Management Education at the Harvard Business School and Boston University (School of Management) in the USA.

REFERENCES

1. Brahm, Ajahn. *Opening the Door of Your Heart*: Brahm Education Centre Ltd, 2004.

2. Canfield, Jack and Chee, Peter. *Coaching for Breakthrough Success: Proven Techniques for Making Impossible Dreams Possible*: McGraw-Hill, 2013.

3. Dweck, Carol S. *Mindset: The New Psychology of Success*: Ballatine Books, 2016.

4. Leong, Wai K. *Empowering Asian Mindsets through Coaching: Discover the secrets of empowerment using the nine coaching mindsets*: Pelanduk Publications (M) Sdn Bhd, 2010.

5. Whitmore, John. *Coaching for Performance: GROWing human potential and purpose*: Nicholas Brealey Publishing, 2015.